WINNING

The race to independent reading ability.

A fast-paced motivational How-to Read, Write and Spell English Program for pre-teens to adults of all ages. Based upon the highly successful Sing, Spell, Read & Write Language Arts Program, WINNING'S songs, games and four student books take non-readers to independent reading ability in 36 steps.

BREAKAWAY
Instructor's Manual
and
Student Book/Answer Keys
(yellow pages)

by Sue Dickson

St. Petersburg, FL 33716

Printed in the United States of America

BREAKAWAY
TABLE OF CONTENTS

Part 1 — Instructor's Manual — Milepost 2-15

BREAKAWAY
The Winning Literacy Program Book #2
Milepost #2 through Milepost #15

Breakaway objectives are:

1. To test student knowledge of consonant and short vowel sounds A to Z.

2. To have student(s) learn the "five most important letters in the alphabet".

3. To have student(s) learn to slide letter sounds together to make "parts of words".

4. To have student(s) read, write, and spell hundreds of short vowel words "automatically".

5. To have student(s) read stories with cumulative vocabularies using these words.

6. To give student(s) Vocabulary Tests, Word Comprehension Tests and Story Comprehension Tests* to determine their percentage of mastery score(s).

Each lesson should provide time to review some or all of the previously taught learn-to-read songs. This will put the knowledge into "long-term memory" and mastery.

Introduction To Milepost #2:

INSTRUCTOR: Read or say, in your own words, to your tutoring student or class.

"Congratulations! As a member of the Winning Team you are now ready for Milepost 2 and the bicycle race. Get the Breakaway student book with bicycle racers pictured on the front cover and let's begin. Milepost 2 is found on page 2. Turn to it."

*Fact and Detail, Sequencing, Main Idea, Predicting Outcome, Opinion, Literal and Inferential Items.

MILEPOST 2 — ABC Echoes

OBJECTIVE

To check each student's ability to say a sound for each letter without looking at the Phonics Song A to Z pictures.

MATERIALS

1. Class Instructors: Manuscript Writing Wall Chart and Breakaway, pages 2-8.
2. Tutors: Breakaway pages 2-8.
3. Blue cassette, Band 2.

PROCEDURE

For Class Instructors and Tutors: Teach your student(s) using the classroom Manuscript Writing Wall Chart marked Milepost 2 (or page 3 of Breakaway). This alphabet strip should be displayed from "A" to "Z" in full view of the class on a side or back wall. This step will serve as further sound-symbol reinforcement and will provide a check of each student's ability to recall the sounds of the letters as learned in "Phonics Song A to Z", without the aid of the pictures this time. The instructor should use a pointer. Tell your student(s) to keep their eyes at the tip of the pointer and to echo after you as you go along the alphabet from "A" to "Z", pointing to the letters, saying each sound as learned in "Phonics Song A to Z". (**Listen to the cassette to hear "ABC Echoes"**.)

> Instructor: (Pointing to Aa) "ă!"
> Student: "ă!"
> Instructor: (Pointing to Bb) "bh!"
> Student: "bh!"
> Instructor: (Pointing to Cc) "ck!"
> Student: "ck!"

Continue along the alphabet saying each sound quickly so you'll leave off the too easily added "ŭ" which does not belong! After you lead the class through the sounds from "A" to "Z", you should ask whether anyone thinks he could point and lead the class as you did through all the sounds. Allow each one to have a turn being leader. Continue practicing this daily until each student can lead the echoes through the alphabet quickly.

Students may do pages 3-8 independently as you listen to individual students say Step 2 echoes. They should also practice writing the alphabet in the space provided on page 2.

(Also, see yellow student book pages 3 — 8 for answer key.)

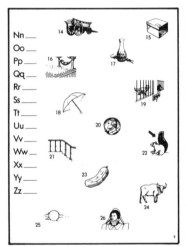

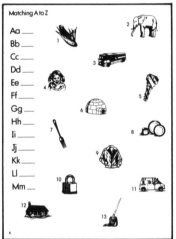

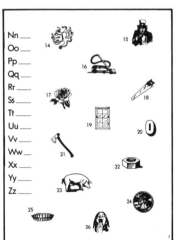

ANSWER KEY, Pages 3-8

Page 3

oxygen(o) alligator(a) web(w) envelope(e) ink(i)
motorcycle(m) desk(d) bell(b) towel(t) foot(f)
kangaroo(k) gas can(g) underline(u) box(x) judge(j)
coins(c) needle(n) paw(p) hand(h) rhinoceros(r)
lighthouse(l) valentine(v) yacht(y) question mark (q)
snowman(s) zipper(z)

Page 4			Page 5		
Aa	7	apple	Nn	20	nickel
Bb	8	ball	Oo	24	ox
Cc	12	cat	Pp	23	pickle
Dd	10	doll	Qq	26	queen
Ee	13	egg	Rr	21	rail
Ff	11	fan	Ss	25	sun
Gg	1	goat	Tt	22	tail
Hh	4	hand	Uu	18	umbrella
Ii	5	Indian	Vv	17	vase
Jj	2	jam	Ww	14	wagon
Kk	3	king	Xx	15	box
Ll	6	lamb	Yy	16	yard
Mm	9	man	Zz	19	zoo

Page 6			Page 7		
Aa	11	ambulance	Nn	22	nut
Bb	3	bus	Oo	14	octopus
Cc	1	corn	Pp	23	pig
Dd	8	dishes	Qq	24	quarter
Ee	2	elephant	Rr	17	rose
Ff	7	fork	Ss	18	saw
Gg	4	girl	Tt	25	teeth
Hh	12	house	Uu	15	Uncle Sam
Ii	6	igloo	Vv	16	vacuum
Jj	9	jacket	Ww	19	window
Kk	5	key	Xx	21	ax
Ll	10	lock	Yy	26	yawn
Mm	13	mop	Zz	20	Zero

ANSWER KEY, Page 8

umpire (u) pillow (p) elevator (e) taxi (x) dog (d)
marbles (m) rug (r) jeep (j) ant (a) book (b)
yo-yo (y) watch (w) hanger (h) ostrich (o) car (c)
invitation (i) fish (f) gum (g) vegetable (v) zebra (z)
nail (n) suit (s) kite (k) turtle (t) ladder (l) quill (q)

"Pass" the students who know the sounds
by initialing and dating the box
provided at the bottom of page 3.
Have students shade in Milepost 2 on the
chart on the inside front cover. Continue
playing games of Sound-O and Pick-A-Sound.

MILEPOST 3 — The Short Vowel Song

OBJECTIVE
1. To teach that there are five letters of the alphabet more important than any others: "Aa", "Ee", "Ii", "Oo" and "Uu"
2. To teach that letters "Aa", "Ee", "Ii", "Oo" and "Uu" are known as **Vowels** (All the rest of the letters are known as **Consonants**.)
3. To teach that the SHORT VOWEL SOUNDS of "Aa", "Ee", "Ii", "Oo" and "Uu" are the sounds we learned when we sang those letters in "Phonics Song A to Z" (There are also **Long** Vowel Sounds for "Aa", "Ee", "Ii", "Oo" and "Uu" that we will earn later in Milepost #18.)
4. To teach that a scooped mark (˘) over a vowel means "to say the short vowel sound"
5. To provide extra short-vowel-sound practice by singing "The Short Vowel Song"

MATERIALS
Classroom: Short Vowel Cards
Tutors: Breakaway, page 9
Blue Cassette, Band 3

PROCEDURE
Have students cut letters from page 9.
Class instructors and tutors introduce this step to everyone at once. Hold up, one by one, the cards with a vowel (a, e, i, o, u) printed on each. Tell the students that these letters are very important letters and that we call them "vowels". Hold up the one with a printed "a" on it and ask the students what sound they have learned for this letter.

> Class: "ă!"

Now, continue in the same manner with each of the other vowel cards, having the class identify each sound. Then, tell the students that you're going to say a sound **four times** and that you want them to tell you the picture they have learned for that sound, as:

Instructor:	"Ă,ă,ă,ă!"
Students:	"apple!"
Instructor:	"Ĕ,ĕ,ĕ,ĕ!"
Students:	"egg!"
Instructor:	"Ĭ, ĭ, ĭ, ĭ!"
Students:	"Indian!"
Instructor:	We're moving as we sing, — (see I'm teaching you a song) "Ŏ,ŏ,ŏ,ŏ!"
Students:	"ox!"
Instructor:	And if there is more than one ox, we say oxen — say it here.
Students:	"oxen!"
Instructor:	Now, we are going to say the next sound only once — listen — "ŭ", umbrella, too.
Students:	"ŭ", umbrella, too.
Instructor:	These are all the short vowel sounds, and you can sing them, too!

Instructor: Wonderful! Now, I want you to notice the little scooped mark over each vowel. It is called the "short vowel mark" and the sounds we have learned are the "short vowel sounds". Now, in order to pass Milepost 3, we are going to learn to sing the "Short Vowel Song". I need five people to line up, one behind the other, in front of this desk (in center front of group and on which the short vowel cards are spread out, face up). I'll go first this time to show you how to do it. Turn on tape of the Short Vowel Song and listen as the vocalists on the tape sing:

"ă,ă,ă,ă" apple	—	Instructor should hold up the "a" card for the class to see.
"ĕ,ĕ,ĕ,ĕ" egg	—	Instructor should hold up the "e" card for the class to see.
"ĭ, ĭ, ĭ, ĭ" Indian	—	Instructor should hold up the "i" card for the class to see.
We're moving as we sing!		
"ŏ,ŏ,ŏ,ŏ" oxen	—	Instructor should hold up the "o" card for the class to see.
"ŭ", umbrella, too!	—	Instructor should hold up the "u" card for the class to see.

These are all the short vowel sounds and you can sing them, too!

The next person in line should step up to take his turn holding up the right vowel cards in sequence as the entire group joins in with the cassette which plays the song five times. Continue in this way until everyone has a turn holding up the cards.

The instructor may want to rearrange cards quickly on the desk after each person's turn to see if the student is capable of choosing the correct card.

After everyone has had a "turn", you can let the students open the Breakaway student book to Milepost 3 and follow along, pointing as they sing. Then have them cut short vowel "cards" from the bottom of the page and all participate holding up their own "cards" as they sing. Listen and watch as each student sings and points. Initial and date the appropriate box. Have students shade in Milepost 3 on the chart on the inside front cover. The students are ready to begin Milepost 4.

Ferris Wheel Song

MILEPOST 4

OBJECTIVES

1. To teach student(s) to slide together or blend two letters (one consonant and one short vowel) to make the "beginnings of words"
2. To **practice** blending two sounds in preparation for reading and spelling hundreds of short vowel words (It is estimated that 62% of the English language is made up of short vowel words and syllables.)

MATERIALS

Class Instructors: Ferris Wheel Chart and Tickets with symbols (☆ □ ○ △)
       Also Breakaway, pages 10 and 11
Tutors: Breakaway, pages 10 and 11
Class Instructors and Tutors: Yellow Cassette, Side 1, "Ferris Wheel Song". Use with tickets
       (☆ □ ○ △)
Yellow Cassette, Side 2, "Ferris Wheel Blends Song". Use with tickets (◁ ⌂ ♡)

TUTOR PREPARATION

1. Remove page 11 and have student(s) cut tickets apart.
2. Arrange tickets in 7 piles by symbols (☆ □ ○ △) and (◁ ⌂ ♡).
3. Now stack each pile by the numbers 1 to 5.
4. Use the "Ferris Wheel" on page 10 on desk top. Use it in place of the "Classroom Chart" in following directions.

CLASSROOM PREPARATION

1. Place the chart-sized Ferris Wheel near the **left front** (**not center front**) of the classroom. This is important.
2. Write numbers #1 to 5 on the floor with chalk as shown.

PROCEDURE

Class Instructors and Tutors: Point to the vowels around the Ferris Wheel Chart and have students tell you the short vowel sounds they learned for each. Sing the Short Vowel Song (to interlock with the last step), pointing from lower left "a" to "u" at the top. Now pick up the ticket with the star symbol #1 and the pointing arrow. With it, point to each vowel going clockwise from lower left "a" and sing the sounds of the vowels up the scale five notes and back down the scale 5 notes, sustaining the sound of each ăăă, ĕĕĕ, etc. Listen to the "Ferris Wheel Song" on tape to hear this if you don't know how it sounds to go up the scale and down.

Pick up star ticket #2 (with letter "b") and ask for the sound of "b". Tell the students, "We're going to learn to put two sounds together by 'Riding the Ferris Wheel' and we'll be making the beginnings of words as we 'ride' and sing."

Instructor:	(Holding "b" ticket) What is the sound of "b"?
Class:	"bh!"
Instructor:	(Pointing to letter "a" on Ferris Wheel) What is the sound of letter "a"?
Class:	"ă!"
Instructor:	(Holding "b" ticket to left of the "a" on Ferris Wheel) Let's say the sound of "b" first, then slide to the "ă" sound. Ready? Watch! Bh...ă! Now, put them together!
Class:	"bă!"
Instructor:	Great! Can anyone think of a word that begins with "bă"?
Class:	"bat!"

Instructor:	Yes, and what do you hear on the end of "bat"?
Class:	"t!"
Instructor:	Can anyone write "bat" on the chalkboard for us?
Student:	(Writes b-a-t)
Instructor:	Great! See, we're reading and spelling words already, and there's no guesswork about it! Does anyone know another word that begins with "ba"?
Student:	"Bag!" (or "bad")
Instructor:	Yes, and what do you hear at the end of "bag" ("bad")?
Student:	"g" (or "d")!

If a student suggests a longer word, as "bath" or "basket", tell them that they are right and we will learn to spell those longer words later.

Instructor: The next ticket I'm going to show you is tricky. Look. Because "C" and "K" have the same sound, they are on opposite sides of the same ticket. You must flip the ticket over as you move it around the Ferris Wheel...so that "c" appears with the "a", "o" and "u"; and "k" is with the "e" and "i". (This is because the "c" gives the "s" sound before "e" and "i" as in **ce**nt and **ci**rcus; but don't go into this with the students now!) Say that we flip the ticket because the words **k**itten and **k**ettle start with "k", and **c**at, **c**ot and **c**ut begin with "c". Tell them: **Just remember: k goes with e and i."**

Continue using different "tickets" in front of the different vowels to let students begin to see and understand the sound-symbol-word-reading-writing relationship.

Now it is time to practice letter-blending with the "Ferris Wheel" song (Yellow Cassette, Side 1).

CLASS INSTRUCTORS
1. Distribute the tickets (with star, box, circle, and triangle symbols) to the students.
2. Tell students to notice the symbols in the corner of each ticket.
3. Show the students the row of symbols (☆ □ ○ △) which are printed across the Ferris Wheel Chart. Tell them to notice that the star is first, the square next, circle next, and then the triangle, from left to right. Tell them this is the order in which they will be used to "ride" the Ferris Wheel. Say: There are five of you who have stars in the corners of your tickets. You will ride first. When the music begins, come to the front and stand on the number matching the number in your star. This will keep the tickets and music together.
   When the "star ticket" people are finished, there is a chorus during which the five students with the box symbol come to stand on their numbers and "ride", etc.

SUMMARY
Each of the "riders" during his turn should:
a. Hold the ticket in left hand as shown, with arm outstretched so all can see the ticket as they sing.
b. Start at the lower left vowel box with "a".
c. Move ticket clockwise, always holding it to the left of the vowel boxes.

Tell students: Everyone should sing together with the Ferris Wheel Song. This will teach the students to blend consonants and short vowel sounds in preparation for reading hundreds of words.

TUTORS
Turn on the cassete and have students sing with the tape using the star (☆) tickets #1

to 5 first, then continuing in the order shown on the Ferris Wheel, using tickets with the symbols (☐ ○ △). This will keep the tickets in the order of the recorded music. Continue reading these directions.

CLASS INSTRUCTORS AND TUTORS

Sing with the Ferris Wheel Song on tape:

> Round and round, and up and down the Ferris Wheel we go.
> Round and round, and up and down; come on now, don't be slow.
> Have your ticket in your hand; the ride will soon begin.
> Do your best, your very best; go round and round again.

First sing the vowels (only) with the arrow #1 ticket. Then with the b ticket, sing:
> "ba", "be", "bi", "bo", "bu"; "bu", "bo", "bi", "be", "ba"

Next, "c" and "k" (Flip the ticket so "k" is with "e" and "i").

Continue in this way with all the tickets, practicing daily. When students are proficient, go on to the Ferris Wheel Blends Song using the tickets with the bell, house, and heart symbols. Ask someone to identify the "br" sound as you hold up that ticket. Do not allow "ber" as acceptable. We do not say berrush (brush) or berroom (broom). Elicit "brh" as the sound for "br". Do the same for "tr". It's "trh" truck, not "terruck". This will help them with spelling later. (Only "er", "ir", "ur", can say "er", not "r" alone.)

CLASS INSTRUCTORS
WORKBOOK DIRECTIONS

After the students have learned to use the large classroom Ferris Wheel, they may practice with their own Ferris Wheel and tickets in Breakaway. Students should cut out the tickets, being careful to keep "c" and "k" tickets joined on the fold as shown. Arrange tickets in seven stacks by symbols and numbers.

CLASS INSTRUCTORS AND TUTORS

When the students are ready to be individually tested on the Ferris Wheel (usually after a week or two of daily practice), call upon them one at a time to use the Ferris Wheel to say or sing each ticket for you. In large classes, it is helpful to hear all students do "star" tickets on Monday, and sign the star in their Breakaway student book. On Tuesday, do the "square" tickets; Wednesday, the "circle" tickets, etc. It takes seven days, but it's very important. Stay with it until they master it. **It is not essential for a student to be able to carry a tune to do this step. The goal is to blend letter sounds**. Sign off and date in symbols at bottom of page when student demonstrates proficiency.

BEGINNING BLENDS SOUNDS, Pages 13, 14 and 15

Have students fill in the correct letter blends for each picture. Upon completion of this step, have the students shade in Milepost 4 on the inside front cover.

(Also, see yellow student book
pages 13 — 15 for answer key.)

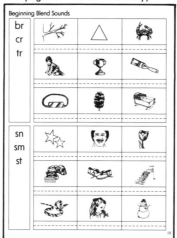

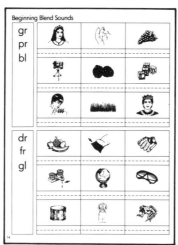

Page 13

branch (br)	triangle (tr)	crab (cr)
crawl (cr)	trophy (tr)	brush (br)
bracelet (br)	tree (tr)	cradle (cr)

stars (st)	smile (sm)	stem (st)
smoke (sm)	sneekers (sn)	stairs (st)
snake (sn)	smell (sm)	snowman (sn)

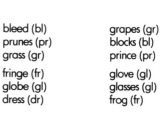

Page 14

princess (pr)	bleed (bl)	grapes (gr)
grill (gr)	prunes (pr)	blocks (bl)
blow (bl)	grass (gr)	prince (pr)

fruit (fr)	fringe (fr)	glove (gl)
drip (dr)	globe (gl)	glasses (gl)
drum (dr)	dress (dr)	frog (fr)

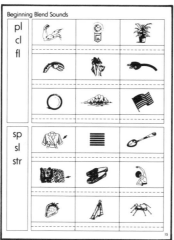

Page 15

flex (fl)	clock (cl)	plant (pl)
claw (cl)	flowers (fl)	plug (pl)
plate (pl)	clouds (cl)	flag (fl)

sleeve (sl)	stripes (str)	spoon (sp)
spots (sp)	slippers (sl)	stretch (str)
strawberry (str)	slide (sl)	spider (sp)

MILEPOST 5 — Short "a" Words

OBJECTIVE
To read the Short "a" Words....Total 59
To have student(s) read, write, spell and understand the meaning of (59) short "a" words

MATERIALS
Class Instructors: The Short "a" Word Chart and Breakaway, pages 16 and 17
Tutors: Breakaway, pages 16 and 17

PROCEDURE
Using the large chart to introduce this step to the class, point to the key letter and picture at the top of the chart. Tutors use page 16 of Breakaway.

Instructor:	Can anyone tell me why this is called the short "a" chart?
Student:	Because there is an "a" in each word on the chart.
Instructor:	Yes! And now, we're going to read some of these short "a" words. I'm going to cover the last letter in the top word, so that we can just see the first two letters — "h...a". Now, what did we say on the Ferris Wheel when we saw these letters? (Thus interlocking the previous step.)
Student:	"hă".
Instructor:	Right! Now, let's say "hă" and then add the sound of this last letter to hear what the word is, OK? "hă...mm". Together, "ham". Yes, "ham". I had a ham sandwich. Now, let's try the next one. What did we say on the Ferris Wheel for "d...a"?
Student:	"dă".
Instructor:	Right! Now, let's add the last sound. What is it? "dă...d". Put it all together now. "dad". He is my dad.

Say each word in a sentence after the students decode it, so that they will enjoy the full meaning. Also, tell students to keep their voices going all the way to the end of the word, blending the letter sounds together, not breaking the word into individual sounds.

Read together all words on the chart (or page). Tell students that there are some words with four letters on this step. For those **longer words**, they must decode the first three letters and then add the final sound. They will read, write, and spell these short "a" words for Milepost 5.

ă

1 ham	13 nap	25 pat
2 dad	14 tag	26 and
3 mat	15 gas	27 fat
4 Dan	16 sad	28 Sam
5 wag	17 bat	29 tap
6 lap	18 can	30 am
7 rag	19 cat	31 fan
8 hat	20 wax	32 mad
9 pan	21 jam	33 bag
10 map	22 pal	34 at
11 man	23 ran	35 bad
12 rat	24 had	36 tax

TIPS FOR STUDENTS:

* Tell the students that for words with "ss", "zz", and "ll" on the end, say the sound only once. Tell them "c" and "k" both have the same sound, so we say the sound just once when "ck" comes together in a word, as in pi**ck**.

* Explain the "e" on the end of "have" is silent, so we have put a strike mark through it. Teach "**s**" taking the "z" sound on "has" and "as". Teach the article "a" as sounding like "ŭ". Bars over a word mean that some letter is "stealing" another letter's sound!

* To assist in the oral spelling of words with four letters, draw four horizontal lines on a card and have the student say the word, sound it out, pointing to a horizontal line for each letter. Have him spell it out before he writes it.

* Have students sound out (decode) each word as they write it in Breakaway.

Practice reading the words on this step in class. Have each student keep his finger on the words as, one by one, each student takes a turn reading a word and using it in a sentence. Then have students read, write, and spell the words **independently** to you and/or another student. Initial and date in the appropriate boxes. **Have the students shade in Milepost 5 on the inside front cover. Tell them they now know how to read, write and spell 59 words!**

Short "a" Stories

OBJECTIVE
To have student(s) read and understand stories with short "a" words

MATERIALS
Breakaway Stories: **"Al and Nat"**, pages 18-21
       "A Man, Pal and Sam", pages 22-24
       "Cal, Pat and Dan", pages 25-28
       Word Recognition and Comprehension, page 29
       Story Comprehension, pages 30 and 31

PROCEDURE
Explain to the class that they will be reading 3 stories. These stories contain only those words they have learned in Milepost 5. Have students volunteer to read aloud to the class. If a student reads a word improperly, the correct response from the instructor should be, "Not (whatever the word was miscalled). Look at the first sound again."

   Instructor: Not "bat". Look at the first sound again.
   Student: "cat".

NEVER TELL the student a word! You may tell him to sound it again — or remind him that the word is a rule breaker or whatever, but let him do the DECODING. Do not direct him to look at the picture for a clue! That is exactly what the old sight-reading method advocated, creating the problem many people have today, where they "look and guess". For example, "bucket" is called "pail" or "birthday" is called "party".

We want ACCURATE READING, no looking and guessing! Each student should be asked to tell in his own words what happened after he reads a page.

   Instructor: Tell us about it, John.

This should follow each student's turn reading. It is the best method of checking comprehension. No "test know-how" is necessary. Students should take Breakaway home to read and practice after they have read in class. They should read each story two or three times until they read it easily — before they are "passed" to the next milepost.

All story reading in "Winning" should follow this procedure.

READING COMPREHENSION TIPS

1. REMEMBER
 To be certain that your learner is reading with understanding, say, "Tell me about it," as he finishes reading each page right from the outset. The learner will "think about what he is reading" if he is asked to "tell about it" immediately after reading it and will not become a "word caller" with a wandering mind. The main purpose of reading is to gain understanding.

2. VOCABULARY
 Be sure your learner readily identifies the words and knows their meanings.

3. GROUP WORDS TOGETHER IN CLUSTERS

Tell students to group the words in clusters to make them "sound like talking". (Do not tell them to "read smoothly!") Practice grouping words in clusters the way we talk, as follows: (Remember to pronounce "the" as "thŭ", and "a" as "ŭ".)

(thŭ)	(ŭ)	(thŭ)	(ŭ)	(thŭ	(ŭ)
the ball	a fox	the box	a cup	the bat	a bed

Learners should practice reading the above list until the two words sound as if they are one word.

Continue with grouping:

> The bat fell to the floor.
> The boy had a cat.

4. OBEY PUNCTUATION

Tell student(s) to obey the "stop signs" of reading .... the punctuation marks.

(.) Periods - Teach the learner to stop at periods, and to start fresh for the next sentence. (Stop completely and shift gears before going on.)

(,) Commas - Teach the learner to pause for a comma. (Tap the brakes quickly.)

(?) Question Mark - Teach the learner to raise his voice at question marks to make it sound as if someone is asking a question. Practice asking questions.

(") Quotation Marks - Teach the learner to raise his voice when reading words that are between quotation marks to make it sound "alive" — as if someone is talking.

(!) Exclamation Point - Teach the learner that an exclamation point is used after such words as "Help!" or "Hurrah!" or other exciting statements as "Fire! Fire!" Teach him to say these words with great feeling.

5. GET BACKGROUND INFORMATION ON TOPIC BEING READ

There is an additional reason why learners may have trouble understanding what they read, even when they know the words and can read with expression: They may not have any experience with what they are reading about. For example, if I, a teacher, were to read a technical book about nuclear engineering, I most certainly would have difficulty understanding it. Although I could read the words and could perhaps even read with expression, I would need someone to EXPLAIN and perhaps to SHOW ME what I read about to help me understand it. This is quite different from someone teaching me what the words are. It is a case of **Reading to Learn** rather than **Learning to Read**. Obviously, **Learning to Read** must come first. (It is an error to try to **Read to Learn** before mastering **Learning to Read**.)

6. READ ALOUD WITH EXPRESSION

Learners should be encouraged to read aloud until they read well with fluency and expression. Until learners can do this, silent reading will be little more than page-staring, picture-looking, and "guessing" to get the "meaning from the page."

Unfortunately, teachers have sometimes been led to believe that a student "reads better silently" if his standardized test scores are adequate for Reading Comprehension. Please remember that a total non-reader can sometimes "get lucky" and without reading one word on a test, fill in the right dots! This may be the reason so many students have "slipped through the cracks" in our education system and graduated from high school illiterate. Remember, **if he cannot read it aloud, he cannot read it**.

WORD RECOGNITION AND COMPREHENSION

"a" Word Recognition, page 29.

Students should be directed to look at the words in box #1. Have them circle the word you pronounce. "Circle the word **fan**. Now look at the words in box #2. Circle the word **tag**."

Call out the words listed below. Say each word distinctly and with emphasis upon the initial and final consonants.

"Circle the word. . ."

1. fan	2. tag	3. at	4. Nat
5. and	6. map	7. van	8. pass
9. and	10. fan	11. fat	12. rag
13. man	14. hand	15. last	16. Al
17. lap	18. ham	19. had	20. Pam

Record the Word Recognition Score, the number correct in the space provided. Compute the Mastery Score (expressed in percentage of mastery) as indicated, and record in the box.

"a" Word Comprehension, page 29.

Tell the students to look at the words in box #1 again and to listen as you read sentences to them. Have them **underline the word that (is)**:

1. something you use when playing baseball
2. the name for a member of the family
3. what you might call a friend
4. what is used to polish a car
5. the word that means to be happy
6. a man's name
7. something used for cooking food
8. the word that means a short sleep
9. something used to carry things
10. a kind of meat that comes from pigs
11. describes the movement of a dog's tail
12. something we eat on toast
13. the word that means naughty
14. something that is found at the seashore
15. the word that means to be quick
16. the word that tells how a person moved quickly
17. what you might say to get a cat to go away
18. a kind of music
19. the word meaning you held something
20. what you put in a car to make it run

Record the Word Comprehension Score (expressed in percentage of mastery) in the space provided.

ANSWER KEY, Page 29

1. bat	2. Dad	3. pal	4. wax
5. glad	6. Sam	7. pan	8. nap
9. bag	10. ham	11. wag	12. jam
13. bad	14. sand	15. fast	16. ran
17. scat	18. jazz	19. had	20. gas

Word Recognition & Comprehension   ă 5

1 cat fan bat	2 tag Dad hat	3 pal at a	4 tax wax Nat
5 cap and glad	6 Sam map tan	7 van mat pan	8 pass nap bass
9 and bag had	10 ham fan man	11 can wag fat	12 jam rag has
13 man bag bad	14 sad hand sand	15 fast last sat	16 ran sat Al
17 tap scat lap	18 mad ham jazz	19 pat had slap	20 Pam nap gas

Word Recognition
Number Correct ____ x 5 =   Mastery Score ___ %

Word Comprehension
Number Correct ____ x 5 =   Mastery Score ___ %

29

(Also, see yellow student book page 29 for answer key.)

(Also, see yellow student book pages 30 and 31 for answer key.)

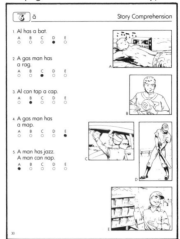

STORY COMPREHENSION

"a" Story Comprehension Test

Story comprehension pages serve as a check of a student's reading comprehension. Have students read the sentences on the left of each page and fill in the circle for the corresponding picture. The sentences and pictures are taken from the stories.

ANSWER KEY, Pages 30 and 31

Page 30

1. D	2. C	3. B	4. E	5. A

Page 31

6. D	7. C	8. E	9. A	10. B

Compute the Story Comprehension Score (expressed in percentage of mastery) and record in the box provided. Students scoring below 80% should repeat the lesson before going on. Have students shade in Milepost 6 on the inside front cover upon completion of this lesson.

MILEPOST 7 | Short "e" Words

OBJECTIVE
To have student(s) read, write, spell and understand the meaning of (60) short "e" words

MATERIALS
Class Instructors: The Short "e" Word Chart and Breakaway, pages 32 and 33
Tutors: Breakaway, pages 32 and 33

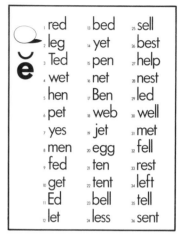

ĕ		
₁ red	₁₃ bed	₂₅ sell
₂ leg	₁₄ yet	₂₆ best
₃ Ted	₁₅ pen	₂₇ help
₄ wet	₁₆ net	₂₈ nest
₅ hen	₁₇ Ben	₂₉ led
₆ pet	₁₈ web	₃₀ well
₇ yes	₁₉ jet	₃₁ met
₈ men	₂₀ egg	₃₂ fell
₉ fed	₂₁ ten	₃₃ rest
₁₀ get	₂₂ tent	₃₄ left
₁₁ Ed	₂₃ bell	₃₅ tell
₁₂ let	₂₄ less	₃₆ sent

PROCEDURE
Using the large chart to introduce this step to the class, point to the key letter and picture at the top of the chart. Tutors use pages 32 and 33 Breakaway.

Instructor: Can anyone tell me why this is called the short "e" chart?

Student: Because there is an "e" in each word on the chart.

Instructor: Yes! And now, we're going to read some of these short "e" words. I'm going to cover the last letter in the top word, so that we can just see the first two letters — "r...e". Now, what did we say on the Ferris Wheel when we saw these letters? (Thus interlocking the previous step.)

Student: "rĕ".

Instructor: Right! Now, let's say "rĕ" and then add the sound of this last letter to hear what the word is, OK? "rĕ...d". Together, "red". Yes, "red". It is painted red. Now, let's try the next one. What did we say on the Ferris Wheel for "l...e"?

Student: "lĕ"

Instructor: Right! Now, let's add the last sound. What is it? "lĕ...g". Put it all together now. "leg". He hurt his leg.

Say each word in a sentence after the students decode it so that they will enjoy the full meaning. Also, tell students to keep their voices going all the way to the end of the word, blending the letter sounds together, not breaking the word into individual sounds.

Read together all words on the chart (or page). Tell students that there are some words with four letters on this step. For those **longer words**, they must decode the first three letters and then add the final sound. They will read, write, and spell these short "e" words for Milepost 7.

Practice reading the words on this step in class. Have each student keep his finger on the words as, one by one, each student takes a turn reading a word and using it in a sentence. Then have students read, write, and spell the words **independently** to you and/or another student. Initial and date in the appropriate boxes. **Have the students shade in Milepost 7 on the inside front cover of Breakaway. Tell them they now know how to read, write and spell 119 words!**

Short "e" Stories

OBJECTIVE
To have student(s) read and understand the story with short "e" words.

MATERIALS
Breakaway Story: **"The Jet"**, pages 34-37.
Word Recognition and Comprehension, page 38
Story Comprehension, pages 39 and 40

PROCEDURE
Explain to the class that they will be reading one story for this step. This story uses only words from the previous lesson (ă words) and those they have just learned in Milepost 7. Have students volunteer to read aloud to the class. If a student reads a word improperly, the correct response from the teacher should be, "Not (whatever the word was miscalled). Look at the first sound again."

Teacher:	Not "leg". Look at the first sound again.
Student:	"beg".

NEVER TELL the student a word! You may tell him to sound it again — or remind him that the word is a rule breaker or whatever, but let him do the DECODING. Do not direct him to look at the picture for a clue! That is exactly what the old sight-reading method advocated, creating the problem many people have today, where they "look and guess". For example "bucket" is called "pail" or "birthday" is called "party".

We want ACCURATE READING, no looking and guessing! Each student should be asked to tell in his own words what happened after he reads a page.
Instructor: Tell us about it, John.

This should follow each student's turn reading. It is your best method of checking comprehension. No "test know-how" is necessary. Students should take Breakaway home to read and practice after they have read in class. They should read each story two or three times until they read it easily — before they are "passed" to the next milepost.

WORD RECOGNITION AND COMPREHENSION

"e" Word Recognition, page 38.

Students should be directed to look at the words in box #1. Have them circle the word that you pronounce. "Circle the word **ten**. Now look at the words in box #2. Circle the word **pet**."

Call out the words listed below. Say each word distinctly and with emphasis upon the initial and final consonants.

"Circle the word. . ."

1. ten	2. pet	3. leg	4. red
5. less	6. Ken	7. sent	8. held
9. yell	10. end	11. fell	12. next
13. get	14. help	15. eggs	16. rest
17. best	18. mend	19. wet	20. fed

Record the Word Recognition Score, the number correct in the space provided. Compute the Mastery Score (expressed in percentage of mastery) as indicated and record in the box.

"e" Word Comprehension, page 38.

Tell the students to look at the words in box #1 again and to listen as you read sentences to them. Have them **underline the word that (is)**:

1. what would you become if water gets spilled on you
2. the color on a traffic signal which means STOP
3. a name for a chicken
4. a kind of airplane
5. the condition of things being sloppy
6. a kind of food usually eaten at breakfast
7. what you use when you write with ink
8. what you do when you assist someone
9. means not straight
10. a place where you might sleep
11. means to speak with a loud voice
12. a home for a bird
13. a part of the body
14. a part of the body between the head and shoulders
15. means gone away
16. something that is finished
17. what happened when someone tripped
18. a number
19. used to answer a question
20. how you feel when you are healthy

Record the Word Comprehension Score (expressed in percentage of mastery) in the space provided.

ANSWER KEY, Page 38

1. wet	2. red	3. hen	4. jet
5. mess	6. egg	7. pen	8. help
9. bent	10. bed	11. yell	12. nest
13. leg	14. neck	15. went	16. end
17. fell	18. ten	19. yes	20. well

Word Recognition & Comprehension

ĕ

1	2	3	4
ten	tell	hen	jet
wet	red	pen	red
let	pet	leg	yes

5	6	7	8
mess	egg	sent	help
less	Ken	peck	mend
left	mess	pen	held

9	10	11	12
bent	end	fell	bent
held	bed	tell	nest
yell	red	yell	next

13	14	15	16
leg	sent	hen	less
get	help	went	rest
gets	neck	eggs	end

17	18	19	20
Peg	mend	wet	nest
best	ten	bed	fed
fell	bent	yes	well

Tell the student to circle the word you call in each box. Have him underline the word referred to in the comprehension question. See manual.

Word Recognition	Mastery Score
Number Correct ___ x 5 =	___ %

Word Comprehension	Mastery Score
Number Correct ___ x 5 =	___ %

(Also, see yellow student book page 38 for answer key.)

(Also, see yellow student book
pages 39 and 40 for answer key.)

STORY COMPREHENSION

"e" Story Comprehension Test

Story comprehension pages serve as a check of a student's reading comprehension. Have students read the sentences on the left of each page and fill in the circle for the corresponding picture. The sentences and pictures are taken from the story.

ANSWER KEY, Pages 39 and 40

Page 39

1. C	2. B	3. E	4. A	5. D

Page 40

6. C	7. A	8. D	9. E	10. B

Compute the Story Comprehension Score (expressed in percentage of mastery), and record in the box provided. Students scoring below 80% should repeat the lesson before going on. Have students shade in Milepost 8 on the inside front cover upon completion of this lesson.

MILEPOST 9 — Short "i" Words

OBJECTIVE
To have student(s) read, write, spell and understand the meaning of (60) short "i" words

MATERIALS
Class Instructors: The Short "i" Word Chart and Breakaway, pages 41 and 42
Tutors: Breakaway, pages 41 and 42

1 him	13 in	25 miss
2 did	14 bit	26 till
3 lip	15 kid	27 Bill
4 win	16 big	28 dig
5 hit	17 it	29 if
6 Tim	18 fix	30 kiss
7 dip	19 wig	31 zip
8 pig	20 six	32 Jim
9 sit	21 hip	33 hill
10 hid	22 lit	34 pin
11 fit	23 Jill	35 rip
12 sip	24 tip	36 will

PROCEDURE
Using the large chart to introduce this step to the class, point to the key letter and picture at the top of the chart. (Tutors, use pages 41 and 42 of Breakaway.)

Instructor: Can anyone tell me why this is called the short "i" chart?

Student: Because there is an "i" in each word on the chart.

Instructor: Yes! And now, we're going to read some of these short "i" words. I'm going to cover the last letter in the top word, so that we can just see the first two letters — "h...i". Now, what did we say on the Ferris Wheel when we saw these letters? (Thus interlocking the previous step.)

Student: "hĭ."

Instructor: Right! Now, let's say "hĭ" and then add the sound of this last letter to hear what the word is, OK? "hĭ...m." Together, "him". Yes, "him". See him run. Now, let's try the next one. What did we say on the Ferris Wheel for "d...i"?

Student: "dĭ."

Instructor: Right! Now, let's add the last sound. What is it? "dĭ...d." Put it all together now. "did." Dan did it.

Say each word in a sentence after the students decode it so that they will enjoy the full meaning. Also, tell students to keep their voices going all the way to the end of the word, blending the letter sounds together, not breaking the word into individual sounds.

Read together all words on the chart (or page). Tell students that there are some words with four letters on this step. For those **longer words**, they must decode the first three letters and then add the final sound. They will read, write, and spell these short "i" words for Milepost 9.

Practice reading the words on this step in class. Have each student keep his finger on the word as, one by one, each student takes a turn reading a word and using it in a sentence. Then have students read, write and spell the words **independently** to you and/or another student. Initial and date in the appropriate boxes. **Have the students shade in Milepost 9 on the inside front cover of Breakaway. Tell them they now know how to read, write and spell 179 words!**

Short "i" Stories

MILEPOST
10

OBJECTIVE
To have student(s) read and understand the stories with short "i" words

MATERIALS
Breakaway Stories: **"Jim, Bill And The Mishap"**, pages 43-45
                     "Kim's Big Win", pages 46-48
                     Word Recognition and Comprehension, page 49
                     Story Comprehension, pages 50 and 51

PROCEDURE
Explain to the class that they will be reading 2 stories. These stories use only words from previous lessons and those they have just learned in Milepost 9. Have students volunteer to read aloud to the class. If a student reads a word improperly, the correct response from the teacher should be, "Not (whatever the word was miscalled). Look at the first sound again."

      Teacher: Not "hit". Look at the first sound again.
      Student: "sit".

NEVER TELL the student a word! You may tell him to sound it again — or remind him that the word is a rule breaker or whatever, but let him do the DECODING. Do not direct him to look at the picture for a clue! That is exactly what the old sight-reading method advocated, creating the problem many people have today, where they "look and guess". For example, "bucket" is called "pail" or "birthday" is called "party".

We want ACCURATE READING, no looking and guessing! Each student should be asked to tell in his own words what happened after he reads a page.

      Teacher: Tell us about it, John.

This should follow each student's turn reading. It is your best method of checking comprehension. No "test know-how" is necessary. Students should take Breakaway home to read and practice after they have read in class. They should read each story two or three times until they read it easily — before they are "passed" to the next milepost.

WORD RECOGNITION AND COMPREHENSION

"i" Word Recognition, page 49.

Students should be directed to look at the words in box #1. Have them circle the word that you pronounce. "Circle the word **if**. Now look at the words in box #2. Circle the word **miss**."

Call out the words listed below. Say each word distinctly and with emphasis upon the initial and final consonants.

"Circle the word. . ."

1. if	2. miss	3. it	4. Sis
5. Jim	6. is	7. milk	8. hit
9. Ripp	10. give	11. did	12. will
13. tin	14. Jim	15. Biff	16. pig
17. fit	18. tip	19. spill	20. is

Record the Word Recognition Score, the number correct in the space provided. Compute the Mastery Score (expressed in percentage of mastery) as indicated and record in the box.

"i" Word Comprehension, page 49.

Tell the students to look at the words in box #1 again and to listen as you read sentences to them. Have them **underline the word that (is)**:

1. to take a small drink
2. a small dog's bark
3. part of the mouth
4. to get gas in your car
5. the animal from which ham comes
6. something to fasten two things together
7. something to keep food off a shirt
8. something to do to a football
9. the cover of a jar or pan
10. what clothes must do on you to look good
11. what to do with a shovel
12. another word for fast
13. what a baseball catcher wears on his hand
14. a woman's name
15. something to give someone you like or love
16. another word for large
17. a drink we get from cows
18. means to pick up something
19. something to give someone on a special occasion
20. the opposite of out

Record the Word Comprehension Score (expressed in percentage of mastery) in the space provided.

ANSWER KEY, Page 49

1. sip	2. yip	3. lip	4. fill
5. pig	6. pin	7. bib	8. kick
9. lid	10. fit	11. dig	12. quick
13. mitt	14. Jill	15. kiss	16. big
17. milk	18. lift	19. gift	20. in

Word Recognition & Comprehension — i 49

1	2	3	4
if	yip	it	six
in	sit	Biff	fill
sip	miss	lip	Sis

5	6	7	8
pig	pin	milk	kick
Jim	is	bib	hit
did	big	hill	jig

9	10	11	12
Ripp	him	dig	will
his	fit	his	bit
lid	give	did	quick

13	14	15	16
mitt	Jill	Biff	pig
digs	Jim	miss	him
tin	will	kiss	big

17	18	19	20
will	whiz	gift	it
milk	tip	spill	is
fit	lift	kiss	in

Tell the student to circle the word you call in each box. Have him underline the word referred to in the comprehension question. See manual.

Word Recognition	Mastery Score	Word Comprehension	Mastery Score
Number Correct ____ x 5 =	%	Number Correct ____ x 5 =	%

(Also, see yellow student book page 49 for answer key.)

(Also, see yellow student book
pages 50 and 51 for answer key.)

STORY COMPREHENSION

"i" Story Comprehension Test

Story comprehension pages serve as a check of a student's reading comprehension.
Have students read the sentences on the left of each page and fill in the circle for the
corresponding picture. The sentences and pictures are taken from the stories.

ANSWER KEY, Pages 50 and 51
Page 50

1. B	2. C	3. D	4. A	5. E

Page 51

6. C	7. A	8. E	9. D	10. B

Compute the Story Comprehension Score (expressed in percentage of mastery) and
record in the box provided. Students scoring below 80% should repeat the lesson before
going on. Have students shade in Milepost 10 on the inside front cover upon completion
of this lesson.

 **Short "o" Words**

OBJECTIVE

To have student(s) read, write, spell and understand the meaning of (60) short "o" words

MATERIALS

Class Instructor: The Short "o" Word Chart and Breakaway, pages 52 and 53
Tutors: Breakaway, pages 52 and 53

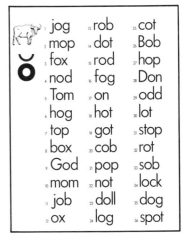

₁ jog	₁₃ rob	₂₅ cot
₂ mop	₁₄ dot	₂₆ Bob
₃ fox	₁₅ rod	₂₇ hop
₄ nod	₁₆ fog	₂₈ Don
₅ Tom	₁₇ on	₂₉ odd
₆ hog	₁₈ hot	₃₀ lot
₇ top	₁₉ got	₃₁ stop
₈ box	₂₀ cob	₃₂ rot
₉ God	₂₁ pop	₃₃ sob
₁₀ mom	₂₂ not	₃₄ lock
₁₁ job	₂₃ doll	₃₅ dog
₁₂ ox	₂₄ log	₃₆ spot

PROCEDURE

Using the large chart to introduce this step to the class, point to the key letter and picture at the top of the chart. Tutors use the chart on pages 52 and 53 of Breakaway.

Instructor:	Can anyone tell me why this is called the short "o" chart?
Student:	Because there is an "o" in each word on the chart.
Instructor:	Yes! And now, we're going to read some of these short "o" words. I'm going to cover the last letter in the top word, so that we can just see the first two letters — "p...o". Now, what did we say on the Ferris Wheel when we saw these letters? (Thus interlocking the previous step.)
Student:	"pŏ."
Instructor:	Right! Now, let's say "pŏ" and then add the sound of this last letter to hear what the word is, OK? "pŏ...t." Together, "pot". Yes, "pot". The pot is black. Now, let's try the next one. What did we say on the Ferris Wheel for "m...ŏ"?
Student:	"mŏ."
Instructor:	Right! Now, let's add the last sound. What is it? "mŏ...p." Put it all together now. "mop." Bring me the mop.

Say each word in a sentence after the students decode it so that they will enjoy the full meaning. Also, tell students to keep their voices going all the way to the end of the word, blending the letter sounds together, not breaking the word into individual sounds.

Read together all words on the chart (or page). Tell students that there are some words with four letters on this step. For those **longer words**, they must decode the first three letters and then add the final sound. They will read, write and spell these short "o" words for Milepost 11.

Practice reading the words on this step in class. Have each student keep his finger on the words as, one by one, each student takes a turn reading a word and using it in a sentence. Then have students read, write and spell the words **independently** to you and/or another student. Initial and date in the appropriate boxes. **Have the students shade in Milepost 11 on the inside front cover of Breakaway. Tell them they now know how to read, write and spell 239 words!**

Short "o" Stories

OBJECTIVE
To have students(s) read and understand the stories with short "o" words

MATERIALS
Breakaway Stories: **"Jack and Jill"**, pages 54 and 55
"Lost!", pages 56-58
Word Recognition and Comprehension, page 59
Story Comprehension, pages 60 and 61

PROCEDURE
Explain to the class that they will be reading 2 stories. These stories use only words from previous lessons and those they have just learned in Milepost 11. Have students volunteer to read aloud to the class. If a student reads a word improperly, the correct response from the teacher should be, "Not (whatever the word was miscalled). Look at the first sound again."

> Instructor: Not "hog". Look at the first sound again.
> Student: "log."

NEVER TELL the student a word! You may tell him to sound it again — or remind him that the word is a rule breaker or whatever, but let him do the DECODING. Do not direct him to look at the picture for a clue! That is exactly what the old sight-reading method advocated, creating the problem many people have today, where they "look and guess". For example "bucket" is called "pail" or "birthday" is called "party".

We want ACCURATE READING, no looking and guessing! Each student should be asked to tell in his own words what happened after he reads a page.
> Teacher: Tell us about it, John.

This should follow each student's turn reading. It is your best method of checking comprehension. No "test know-how" is necessary. Students should take Breakaway home to read and practice after they have read in class. They should read each story two or three times until they read it easily — before they are "passed" to the next milepost.

WORD RECOGNITION AND COMPREHENSION

"o" Word Recognition, page 59.

Students should be directed to look at the words in box #1. Have them circle the word that you pronounce. "Circle the word **fox**. Now look at the words in box #2. Circle the word **box**."

Call out the words listed below. Say each word distinctly and with emphasis upon the initial and final consonants.

"Circle the word. . ."

1. fox	2. box	3. God	4. log
5. dog	6. hot	7. pot	8. hop
9. from	10. lot	11. Todd	12. on
13. sock	14. odd	15. rock	16. doll
17. spot	18. not	19. top	20. blocks

Record the Word Recognition Score, the number correct in the space provided. Compute the Mastery Score (expressed in percentage of mastery) as indicated and record in the box.

"o" Word Comprehension, page 59.

Tell the students to look at the words in box #1 again and to listen as you read sentences to them. Have them **underline the word that (is)**:

1. what a food spill makes on your clothes
2. a very large pig
3. to jump on one foot
4. how you feel when the temperature is high
5. a child's toy
6. another name for Mother
7. a soldier's bed
8. wood to burn in a fireplace
9. to steal
10. a measurement for a small piece of land
11. a kind of drum
12. opposite of bottom
13. an animal kept for a pet
14. the sound of a small explosion
15. something to show us the time
16. something a little strange or different
17. means to halt
18. something to open with a key
19. a small, wild animal
20. a cooking utensil

Record the Word Comprehension Score (expressed in percentage of mastery) in the space provided.

ANSWER KEY, Page 59

1. spot	2. hog	3. hop	4. hot
5. doll	6. Mom	7. cot	8. log
9. rob	10. lot	11. tom-tom	12. top
13. dog	14. pop	15. clock	16. odd
17. stop	18. lock	19. fox	20. pot

Word Recognition & Comprehension ŏ

1 fox top spot	2 rob box hog	3 God hop dot	4 hot got log
5 doll dog jog	6 Mom stop hot	7 not pot cot	8 hop stop log
9 rob hog from	10 ox lot Oz	11 Todd cot tom-tom	12 on lot top
13 log sock dog	14 not pop odd	15 lock clock rock	16 odd on doll
17 pop spot stop	18 rock not lock	19 fox top box	20 sock blocks pot

Tell the student to circle the word you call in each box. Have him underline the word referred to in the comprehension question. See manual.

Word Recognition	Mastery Score	Word Comprehension	Mastery Score
Number Correct ____ x 5 =	____ %	Number Correct ____ x 5 =	____ %

59

(Also, see yellow student book page 59 for answer key.)

29

(Also, see yellow student book
page 60 and 61 for answer key.)

STORY COMPREHENSION
"o" Story Comprehension Test

Story comprehension pages serve as a check of a student's reading comprehension. Have the students read the sentences on the left of each page and fill in the circle for the corresponding picture. The sentences and pictures are taken from the stories.

ANSWER KEY, Pages 60 and 61

Page 60

1. D	2. E	3. B	4. A	5. C

Page 61

6. D	7. A	8. C	9. E	10. B

Compute the Story Comprehension Score (expressed in percentage of mastery) and record in the box provided. Students scoring below 80% should repeat lesson before going on. Have students shade in Milepost 12 on the inside front cover upon completion of this lesson.

Short "u" Words

OBJECTIVE
To have student(s) read, write, spell and understand the meanings of (60) short "u" words

MATERIALS
Class Instructor: The Short "u" Word Chart and Breakaway, pages 62 and 63
Tutors: Breakaway, page 62 and 63

PROCEDURE
Using the large chart to introduce this step to the class, point to the key letter and picture at the top of the chart. Tutors use page 62 of the student book.

Teacher:	Can anyone tell me why this is called the short "u" chart?
Student:	Because there is a "u" in each word on the chart.
Teacher:	Yes! And now, we're going to read some of these short "u" words. I'm going to cover the last letter in the top word, so that we can just see the first two letters — "b...u". Now, what did we say on the Ferris Wheel when we saw these letters? (Thus interlocking the previous step.)
Student:	"bŭ."
Teacher:	Right! Now, let's say "bŭ" and then add the sound of this last letter to hear what the word is, OK? "bŭ...g." Together, "bug". Yes, "bug". A beetle is a bug. Now, let's try the next one. What did we say on the Ferris Wheel for "c...u"?
Student:	"cŭ."
Teacher:	Right! Now, let's add the last sound. What is it? "cŭ...t." Put it all together now. "cut." Cut the paper.

Say each word in a sentence after the students decode it so that they will enjoy the full meaning. Also, tell students to keep their voices going all the way to the end of the word, blending the letter sounds together, not breaking the word into individual sounds.

Read together all words on the chart (or page). Tell students that there are some words with four letters on this step. For those **longer words**, they must decode the first three letters and then add the final sound. They will read, write and spell these short "u" words for Milepost 13.

Practice reading the words on this step in class. Have each student keep his finger on the words as, one by one, each student takes a turn reading a word and using it in a sentence. Then have students read, write and spell the words **independently** to you and/or another student. Initial and date in the appropriate boxes. **Have the students shade in Milepost 13 on the inside front cover of Breakaway. Tell them they now know how to read, write and spell 299 words!**

Short "u" Stories

OBJECTIVE
To have student(s) read and understand the story with short "u" words

MATERIALS
Breakaway Story: **"Bud's Dump Truck"**, pages 64 and 65.

Word Recognition and Comprehension, page 66

Story Comprehension, pages 67 and 68

PROCEDURE
Explain to the class that they will be reading one story. This story uses only words from previous lessons and those they have just learned in Milepost 13. Have students volunteer to read aloud to the class. If a student reads a word improperly, the correct response from the teacher should be, "Not (whatever the word was miscalled). Look at the first sound again."

Instructor: Not "but". Look at the first sound again.

Student: "hut."

NEVER TELL the student a word! You may tell him to sound it again — or remind him that the word is a rule breaker or whatever, but let him do the DECODING. Do not direct him to look at the picture for a clue! That is exactly what the old sight-reading method advocated, creating the problem many people have today, where they "look and guess". For example, "bucket" is called "pail" or "birthday" is called "party."

We want ACCURATE READING, no looking and guessing! Each student should be asked to tell in his own words what happened after he reads a page.

Instructor: Tell us about it, John.

This should follow each student's turn reading. It is your best method of checking comprehension. No "test know-how" is necessary. Students should take Breakaway home to read and practice after they have read in class. They should read each story two or three times until they read it easily — before they are "passed" to the next milepost.

WORD RECOGNITION AND COMPREHENSION

"u" Word Recognition, page 66.

Students should be directed to look at the words in box #1. Have them circle the word that you pronounce. "Circle the word **rub**. Now look at the words in box #2. Circle the word **bug**."

Call out the words listed below. Say each word distinctly and with emphasis upon the initial and final consonants.

"Circle the word. . ."

1. rub	2. bug	3. cup	4. mug
5. fun	6. us	7. fuss	8. tug
9. pup	10. run	11. drum	12. dug
13. hut	14. nut	15. us	16. truck
17. cut	18. hum	19. duck	20. puff

Record the Word Recognition Score, the number correct in the space provided. Compute the Mastery Score (expressed in percentage of mastery) as indicated and record in the box.

"u" Word Comprehension, page 66.

Tell the students to look at the words in box #1 again and to listen as you read sentences to them. Have them **underline the word that (is)**:

1. something that shines in the sky
2. something to crack open and eat
3. a large vehicle for many passengers
4. singing with your lips closed
5. another word for slice
6. opposite of down
7. a soft bread roll
8. a place to send garbage
9. the noise a bee makes
10. means to take a large swallow
11. means to fit tightly
12. another name for an insect
13. what has happened when you can't get out of the mud
14. a mixture of water and dirt
15. something from which you drink
16. something to protect you from the rain
17. a place to take a bath
18. means to hop
19. means you have to do it
20. what an unhappy baby might do

Record the Word Comprehension Score (expressed in percentage of mastery) in the space provided.

ANSWER KEY, Page 66

1. sun	2. nut	3. bus	4. hum
5. cut	6. up	7. bun	8. dump
9. buzz	10. gulp	11. snug	12. bug
13. stuck	14. mud	15. cups	16. umbrella
17. tub	18. jump	19. must	20. fuss

(Also, see yellow student book page 66 for answer key.)

(Also, see yellow student book
pages 67 and 68 for answer key.)

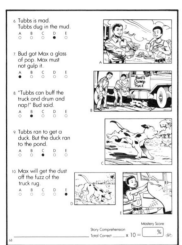

STORY COMPREHENSION
"u" Story Comprehension Test

Story comprehension pages serve as a check of a student's reading comprehension. Have the students read the sentences on the left of each page and fill in the circle for the corresponding picture. The sentences and pictures are taken from the story.

ANSWER KEY, Pages 67 and 68
Page 67

1. E	2. C	3. B	4. A	5. D

Page 68

6. D	7. A	8. B	9. C	10. E

Compute the Story Comprehension Score (expressed in percentage of mastery) and record in the box provided. Students scoring below 80% should repeat the lesson before going on. Have students shade in Milepost 14 on the inside front cover upon completion of this lesson.

MILEPOST 15 "a", "e", "i", "o", "u"
Longer Short Vowel Words

OBJECTIVE
1. To have student(s) read, write, spell and understand the longer "short vowel words"...Total 86
2. To have student(s) read the longer short vowel words in context in a story
3. To test student(s') reading comprehension (end of Milepost 15)

MATERIALS
Breakaway Student book, pages 69-71.

PROCEDURE
Practice reading the words on this step. Have each student keep a finger under the words as, one by one, each student takes a turn to read a word and then uses it in a sentence. Then have the students read, write and spell the words **independently** to you and/or another student. Initial and date the boxes provided. **Tell them they can now read, write and spell 385 words!**

Actually, they can read many more. It is estimated that 62% of the English language is made up of short vowel words and syllables.

MILEPOST 15 STORIES
Read and discuss the following stories from Breakaway student book:
> **"Hot Rod Fix-It Pit Stop,"** pages 72-75
> **"The Junk Stop,"** pages 76-78
> **"The Jazz Band,"** pages 79-81

WORD RECOGNITION AND COMPREHENSION
"a", "e", "i", "o", "u" Word Recognition, page 82

Students should be directed to look at the words in box #1. Have them circle the word that you pronounce. "Circle the word **land**. Now look at the words in box #2. Circle the word **stick**."

Call out the words listed below. Say each word distinctly and with emphasis upon the initial and final consonants.

"Circle the word. . ."

1. land	2. stick	3. sock	4. list
5. dump	6. Jack	7. melt	8. tack
9. desk	10. hunt	11. gulp	12. bend
13. truck	14. block	15. fist	16. sift
17. must	18. pick	19. damp	20. fond

Record the Word Recognition Score, the number correct in the space provided. Compute the Mastery Score (expressed in percentage of mastery) as indicated and record in the box.

15 ă,ĕ,ĭ,ŏ,ŭ	Word Recognition & Comprehension		
1 lump lamp land	2 stick snack spend	3 sand send sock	4 lift list limp
5 dust dump dots	6 just jump Jack	7 melt mend milk	8 test tack tent
9 Dick duck desk	10 hunt hump hand	11 grand gulp gift	12 best bend band
13 truck clock stick	14 belt block bulb	15 fact fast fist	16 sock sick sift
17 must mask mend	18 pill pick pond	19 damp dump duck	20 from frog fond

(Also, see yellow student book page 82 for answer key.)

"a", "e", "i", "o", "u" Word Comprehension, page 82

Tell the students to look at the words in box #1 again and to listen as you read sentences to them. Have them **underline the word that (is):**

1. something you use for light
2. something to eat
3. something you see at the beach
4. something you might do, if you have sprained an ankle
5. small circle-like marks
6. how to move from one place to another
7. something to drink
8. something used for camping
9. a man's name
10. a part of the body
11. something you give to someone
12. a group of musicians
13. something you use to tell time
14. something you wear around your waist
15. a bit of true information
16. something you may wear on your foot
17. to repair or fix
18. a small body of water
19. a bird that lives near water
20. a small green animal known for its hopping ability

Record the Word Comprehension Score (expressed in percentage of mastery) in the space provided.

ANSWER KEY, Page 82

1. lamp	2. snack	3. sand	4. limp
5. dots	6. jump	7. milk	8. tent
9. Dick	10. hand	11. gift	12. band
13. clock	14. belt	15. fact	16. sock
17. mend	18. pond	19. duck	20. frog

(Also, see yellow student book pages 83 and 84 for answer key.)

STORY COMPREHENSION

"a", "e", "i", "o", "u" Story Comprehension Test

Story comprehension pages serve as a check of a student's reading comprehension. Have the students read the sentences on the left of each page and fill in the circle for the corresponding picture. The sentences and pictures are taken from the stories.

ANSWER KEY, Pages 83 and 84

Page 83

1. C	2. E	3. D	4. A	5. B

Page 84

6. C	7. E	8. D	9. B	10. A

Compute the Story Comprehension Score (expressed in percentage of mastery) and record in the box provided. Students scoring below 80% should repeat the lesson before going on. Have students shade in Milepost 15 on the inside front cover upon completion of this lesson.

The students have now completed Breakaway. Fill out the Certificate of Achievement at the end of the student book. You may wish to have a celebration with your students.

The race to independent reading ability.

A fast-paced motivational How-to Read, Write and Spell English Program for pre-teens to adults of all ages. Based upon the highly successful Sing, Spell, Read & Write Language Arts Program, WINNING'S songs, games and four student books take non-readers to independent reading ability in 36 steps.

by Sue Dickson

St. Petersburg, FL 33716

Printed in the United States of America

(ISBN 1-56704-401-8)

A B C Echoes

Say a sound for each letter and practice writing

INITIAL   DATE

2

Beginning Sounds

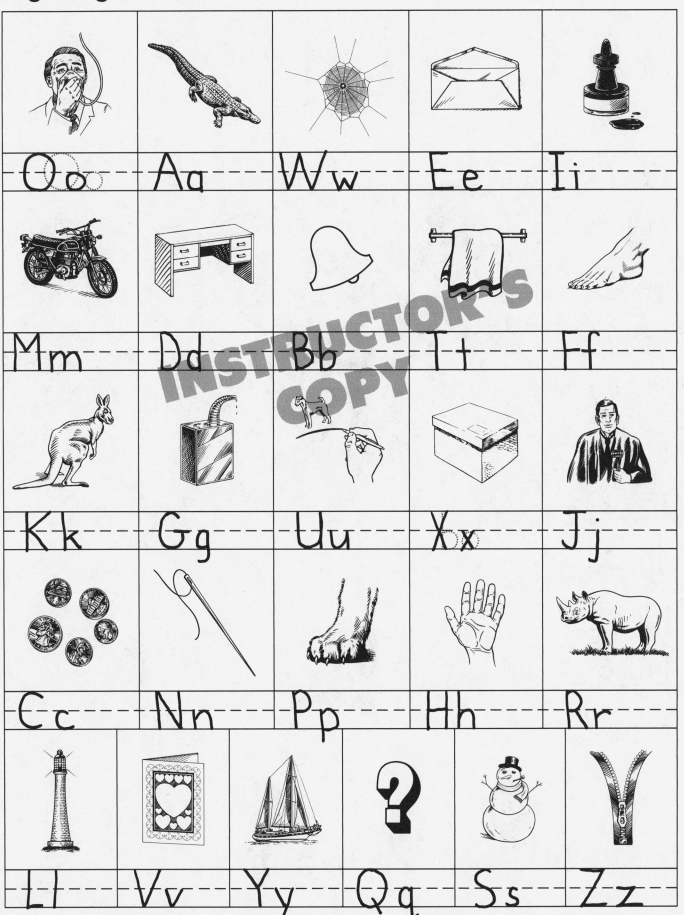

Oo	Aa	Ww	Ee	Ii
Mm	Dd	Bb	Tt	Ff
Kk	Gg	Uu	Xx	Jj
Cc	Nn	Pp	Hh	Rr
Ll	Vv	Yy	Qq	Ss	Zz

3

Matching A to Z

Aa _7_

Bb _8_

Cc _12_

Dd _10_

Ee _13_

Ff _11_

Gg _1_

Hh _4_

Ii _5_

Jj _2_

Kk _3_

Ll _6_

Mm _9_

1

2

3

4

5

6

7

8

9

10

11

12

13

Nn <u>20</u>

Oo <u>24</u>

Pp <u>23</u>

Qq <u>26</u>

Rr <u>21</u>

Ss <u>25</u>

Tt <u>22</u>

Uu <u>18</u>

Vv <u>17</u>

Ww <u>14</u>

Xx <u>15</u>

Yy <u>16</u>

Zz <u>19</u>

14

15

16

17

18

19

20

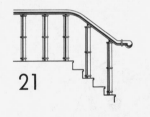

21

22

23

24

25

26

5

Matching A to Z

Aa _11_

Bb _3_

Cc _1_

Dd _8_

Ee _2_

Ff _7_

Gg _4_

Hh _12_

Ii _6_

Jj _9_

Kk _5_

Ll _10_

Mm _13_

1

2

3

4

5

6

7

8

9

10

11

12

13

Nn 22
Oo 14
Pp 23
Qq 24
Rr 17
Ss 18
Tt 25
Uu 15
Vv 16
Ww 19
Xx 21
Yy 26
Zz 20

14

15

16

17

18

19

20

21

22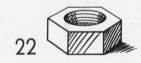

23

24

25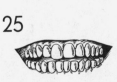

26

7

Beginning Sounds

Uu	Pp	Ee	Xx	Dd
Mm	Rr	Jj	Aa	Bb
Yy	Ww	Hh	Oo	Cc
Ii	Ff	Gg	Vv	Zz
Nn	Ss	Kk	Tt	Ll	Qq

Short Vowel Song

Sing Along and Point

ă, ă, ă, ă, apple

ĕ, ĕ, ĕ, ĕ, egg

ĭ, ĭ, ĭ, ĭ,  Indian

We're moving as we sing.

ŏ, ŏ, ŏ, ŏ, oxen

ŭ,  umbrella too!

These are all the short vowel sounds, and you can sing them too!

INITIAL   DATE

Cut out short vowel cards below and spread out face up on desk. Sing the short vowel song, holding up one by one the correct card.

 ă   ĕ   ĭ   ŏ   ŭ

 Hold tickets in left hand as shown. Start at lower left **a**.
Move tickets clockwise, always holding to left of vowel boxes.
Sing with Ferris Wheel Song on tape.

Initial and date each symbol below when mastered.

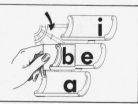

Cut tickets apart, keep k and c as one ticket, folded together. Store tickets in an envelope.

☆ →
☆2 b
k
☆3 c
☆4 d
☆5 f
🔔1 br
🔔2 cr
🔔3 tr

1 g
2 h
j
4
5 m
🔔4 fr
🔔5 dr
🏠1 gr
🏠2 pr

1 n
2 p
3 qu
4 r
5 s
🏠3 bl
🏠4 pl
🏠5 cl
♡1 fl

△1 t
△2 v
△3 w
△4 y
△5 z
♡2 st
♡3 sn
♡4 sm
♡5 str

11

Beginning Blend Sounds

br cr tr			

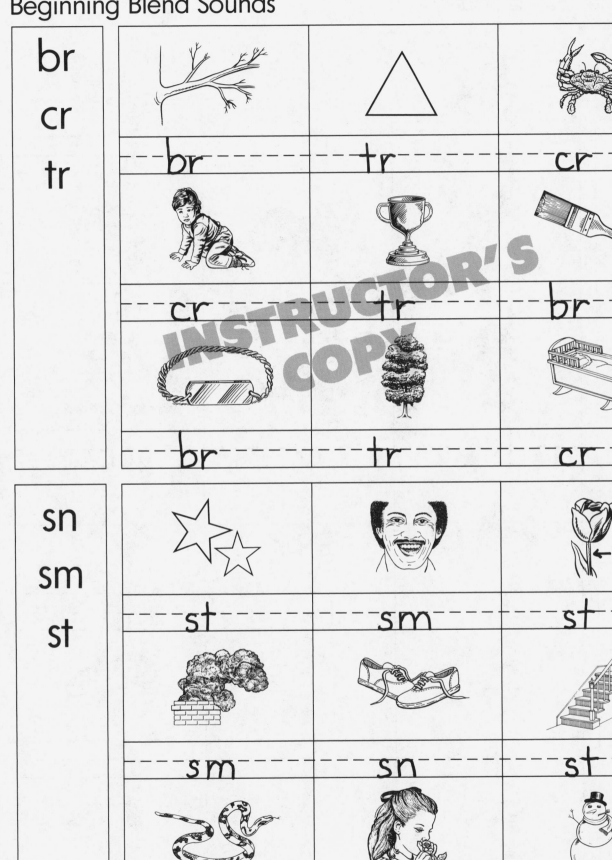

br	tr	cr
cr	tr	br
br	tr	cr

sn sm st			

st	sm	st
sm	sn	st
sn	sm	sn

Beginning Blend Sounds

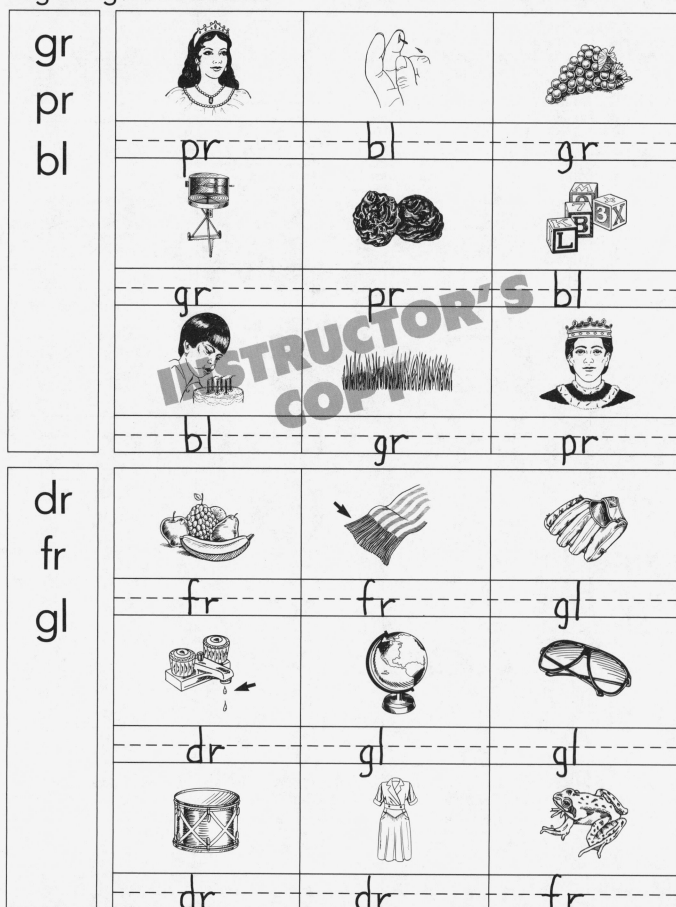

gr pr bl

pr	bl	gr
gr	pr	bl
bl	gr	pr

dr fr gl

fr	fr	gl
dr	gl	gl
dr	dr	fr

Beginning Blend Sounds

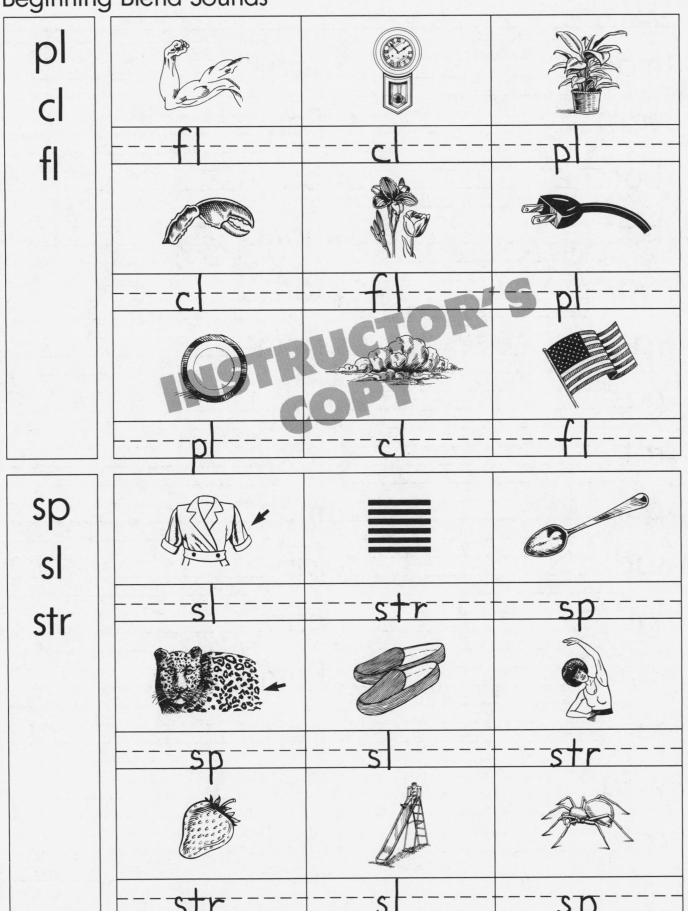

pl cl fl			
	fl	cl	pl
	cl	fl	pl
	pl	cl	fl

sp sl str			
	sl	str	sp
	sp	sl	str
	str	sl	sp

15

1 map   map

2 van

3 bad

4 hat

5 wax

6 ran

7 gas

8 rat

9 pal

10 sad

11 fat

12 tan

13 sat

14 wag

15 cat

16 rag

17 Sam

18 bat

19 ham

20 fan

21 man

22 ask

23 tax

24 mad

25 lap

26 nap

27 Pam

28 bag

29 rap

30 dad

CAN READ	CAN WRITE	CAN SPELL
INITIAL DATE	INITIAL DATE	INITIAL DATE

31 pan

32 mat

33 tap

34 jam

35 pad

36 and

37 tag

38 pat

39 can

40 had

41 cap

42 Dan

43 at

44 Ann

45 Nat

46 am

47 fast

48 bass

49 jazz

50 pass

51 sand

52 last

53 glad

54 scat

55 have

56 (wŭz) was

57 as

58 has

59 a

Tell the students that double letters (ll, ss, etc) on the end of a word, say the sound only once, Ck says the sound only once.

CAN READ	CAN WRITE	CAN SPELL
INITIAL DATE	INITIAL DATE	INITIAL DATE

Al and Nat

Nat has ham.

Al has jam.

Nat has a bag.

Al has a bat.

Al has a hat.

Al can tap a cap.

Nat! Nat! Nat!

Nat has a fan.

Al can fan Nat.

Nat has a van.

A van has gas.

A gas man has a rag.

A gas man has a map.

A man had a bag. A man had a can.

A can had ham.

A man had jam.
A man had ham and jam.

A man has jazz.
A man can nap.

Pal had a nap.

Bad Sam can tag Pal.
..tap...tap...tap.

Pal ran at Sam.

Sam ran.

Pal ran and ran.　　　Sam ran

and ran
and ran.

A man had sand.
Ham had sand.
Jam had sand.

Bad Pal! Bad Sam!

A mad man ran at Pal.

Sam ran fast!
　　Pal ran at Sam.

A man has Pal.
A man has Sam.
A man can tan at last.

Cal, Pat and Dan

Cal has a pal. Cal has lad.
Lad has a pal. Lad has Cal.
Dan has a pal. Dan has Pat.

25

Pat has a pal. Pat has Tab. Tab has a pal. Tab has Pat.

Dan has a van. Cal and Lad sat. Pat and Tab sat.

A man has a map. A man has a rag. A van has gas. Gas has a tax.

Glad Cal. Glad Dan. Glad Pat. Lad and Tab sat.

Cal has a can. Cal has wax. A man can pass Cal and Pat and Dan.

Dan has ham. A man has a fan. Cal has a bass. Pat has a can.

Pat has a cap. Cal has a cap. Dan has a cap. A man has a black hat.

A man has a glass. Dan has a can. Pat has a can. Cal has a can.

Dan has a mat. Pat has a rag. Cal has jam.

Sal has a bag. Sal can pack a bag.

Cal can hand Sal a can and a ham.

Cal can hand Sal jam and wax. Pat can hand Sal rags and a mat.

Fast Sal can bag a cap and a can. Sal packs fast.

Dan has a bag. Dan can pack a van. Pat has a lap. Pat can pat Tab. Cal has a lap. Cal can pat Lad.

Cal has jam. Dan has ham. Pat has ham.

Dan and Cal have caps. Pat has jazz. Dan has a backpack, and Cal has a backpack.

Cal can pass a can.
Lad can pass a can.

Pat can pass a can. Tab can pass a can.

Dan can pass sand.
Mac has sand.

And Tab has sand.

Dan can tap Pat.

At last, Dan has a nap. Cal has a nap. Pat has a nap. Glad Lad. Glad Tab.

28

Word Recognition & Comprehension

1 cat (fan) bat	2 (tag) Dad hat	3 pal (at) a	4 tax wax (Nat)
5 cap (and) glad	6 Sam (map) tan	7 (van) mat pan	8 (pass) nap bass
9 (and) bag had	10 ham (fan) man	11 can wag (fat)	12 jam (rag) has
13 (man) bag bad	14 sad (hand) sand	15 fast (last) sat	16 ran sat (Al)
17 tap scat (lap)	18 mad (ham) jazz	19 pat (had) slap	20 (Pam) nap gas

Tell the student to circle the word you call in each box. Have him underline the word referred to in the comprehension question. See manual.

Mastery Score

Word Recognition

Number Correct _____ x 5 = [%]

Mastery Score

Word Comprehension

Number Correct _____ x 5 = [%]

29

1. Al has a bat.

A ○ B ○ C ○ D ● E ○

A

2. A gas man has a rag.

A ○ B ○ C ● D ○ E ○

3. Al can tap a cap.

A ○ B ● C ○ D ○ E ○

B

4. A gas man has a map.

A ○ B ○ C ○ D ○ E ●

C

D

5. A man has jazz.
A man can nap.

A ● B ○ C ○ D ○ E ○

E

6. A man had ham
   and jam.

   A   B   C   D   E
   ○   ○   ○   ●   ○

A

7. A man can tan at last.

   A   B   C   D   E
   ○   ○   ●   ○   ○

8. Sal has a bag.
   Sal can pack a bag.

   A   B   C   D   E
   ○   ○   ○   ○   ●

B

9. A man has a
   black hat.

   A   B   C   D   E
   ●   ○   ○   ○   ○

C

10. At last, Dan has a nap.
    Cal has a nap. Pat
    has a nap. Glad Lad.
    Glad Tab.

   A   B   C   D   E
   ○   ●   ○   ○   ○

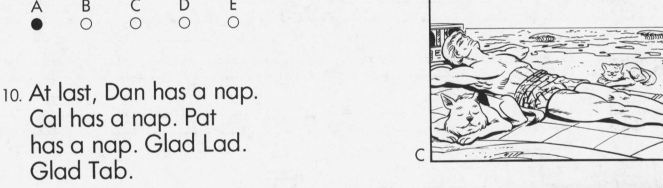

D   E

Mastery Score

Story Comprehension

Total Correct _____ x 10 = [%   ]

1 wet   *wet*

2 let

3 den

4 leg

5 pen

6 pet

7 web

8 get

9 gets

10 red

11 Ken

12 jet

13 men

14 beg

15 ten

16 fed

17 yet

18 pep

19 yes

20 net

21 egg

22 eggs

23 set

24 Ted

25 hen

26 bed

27 Ed

28 Peg

29 less

30 mess

CAN READ	CAN WRITE	CAN SPELL
INITIAL DATE	INITIAL DATE	INITIAL DATE

31 yell

32 well

33 bell

34 fell

35 tell

36 sell

37 bent

38 sent

39 best

40 nest

41 rest

42 went

43 mend

44 held

45 help

46 next

47 left

48 peck

49 neck

50 tend

51 deck

52 met

53 lend

54 step

55 rent

56 dent

57 led

58 bet

59 Ben

60 the

CAN READ	CAN WRITE	CAN SPELL
INITIAL DATE	INITIAL DATE	INITIAL DATE

The Jet

Dad, Peg, and Ken went.
Nat, the cat, went.
The bags went.

Peg has a lap. Nat sat.
Peg can pat Nat's neck
Nat has a bell.

Dad gets the bag.
Ken has a bag.
Peg has Nat, the cat.

The man has tags. The man can tag
the bags. Nat, the cat, gets a tag.

The bags went.
Nat, the cat, went.
Sad Peg. Sad Nat.

The man gets Dad's pass.
The man lets Peg pass.
Ken hands the man a pass.

Peg and Ken sat. Peg and
Ken had a belt. Dad had a
belt.

The jet left the land fast!

Jan has the ham, eggs, and a red can. Peg has ham. Ken has eggs. Dad has a nap.

A can fell. Peg has a red, wet mess. Jan, lend a hand!

Help!

Peg's bag is red and wet. Peg has a mess. Dad's vest has a mess.

Jan has a rag. Jan can help. Peg's hand has less red mess. Peg's bag has less red mess.

Dad's vest is wet.

At last, the jet can land. Tell Dad.

Peg and Ken clap.

Dad left the jet!
Peg and Ken left the jet.

Dad and Ken get the
bags. Peg gets the cat.

Nat sat. Peg's best pet sat.
At last, Peg can rest.

Dad and Ken left. Peg and
Nat left. And the
jet left. FAST!

1 (ten) wet let	2 tell red (pet)	3 hen pen (leg)	4 jet (red) yes
5 mess (less) left	6 egg (Ken) mess	7 (sent) peck pen	8 help mend (held)
9 bent held (yell)	10 (end) bed red	11 (fell) tell yell	12 bent nest (next)
13 leg (get) gets	14 sent (help) neck	15 hen went (eggs)	16 less (rest) end
17 Peg (best) fell	18 (mend) ten bent	19 (wet) bed yes	20 nest (fed) well

Tell the student to circle the word you call in each box. Have him underline the word referred to in the comprehension question. See manual.

Mastery Score

Word Recognition

Number Correct _____ x 5 = [___ %]

Mastery Score

Word Comprehension

Number Correct _____ x 5 = [___ %]

38

Story Comprehension

1. Peg and Ken sat.
   Dad had a belt.
   Peg and Ken had a belt.

   A ○ B ○ C ● D ○ E ○

2. Peg can pat Nat's neck!
   Nat has a bell.

   A ○ B ● C ○ D ○ E ○

3. The man gets Dad's pass.
   The man let Peg pass.
   Ken hands the man a
   pass.

   A ○ B ○ C ○ D ○ E ●

4. A can fell.
   Peg has a red, wet mess.

   A ● B ○ C ○ D ○ E ○

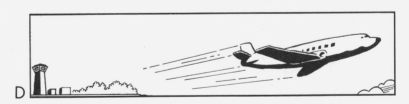

5. The jet left the land, fast!

   A ○ B ○ C ○ D ● E ○

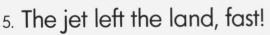

39

6. Dad gets the bag.
   Ken has a bag.

   A   B   C   D   E
   ○   ○   ●   ○   ○

A

7. Peg's bag is red and wet.
   Peg has a mess.
   Dad's vest has a mess.

   A   B   C   D   E
   ●   ○   ○   ○   ○

B

8. The man has tags.
   The man can tag the
   bags. Nat, the cat, gets
   a tag.

   A   B   C   D   E
   ○   ○   ○   ●   ○

C

D

9. Dad and Ken get the
   bags. Peg gets the cat.

   A   B   C   D   E
   ○   ○   ○   ○   ●

10. Dad and Ken left.
    Peg and Nat left.

    A   B   C   D   E
    ○   ●   ○   ○   ○

E

Story Comprehension

Total Correct _____ x 10 =

Mastery Score

%

40

1 pin _pin_

2 pig

3 sip

4 him

5 fit

6 rip

7 bit

8 dip

9 hip

10 Jim

11 dig

12 digs

13 hit

14 big

15 six

16 jig

17 sin

18 it

19 yip

20 sit

21 win

22 fib

23 wig

24 Tim

25 rib

26 lip

27 lid

28 zip

29 in

30 tip

CAN READ

INITIAL   DATE

CAN WRITE

INITIAL   DATE

CAN SPELL

INITIAL   DATE

31 hid

32 if

33 Sis

34 fix

35 bib

36 did

37 lit

38 tin

39 kid

40 mix

41 ill

42 Bill

43 hill

44 Jill

45 pill

46 will

47 fill

48 miss

49 kiss

50 mitt

51 spill

52 quick

53 milk

54 swim

55 lift

56 gift

57 Biff

58 give

59 is

60 his

CAN READ	CAN WRITE	CAN SPELL
INITIAL DATE	INITIAL DATE	INITIAL DATE

Jim, Bill and the Mishap

Jim is big.
Jim is in a red cap.
Jim is in tan track pants.
Jim is fast.

Bill is in red pants.
Bill is quick.
Jim and Bill
    ran and ran.

Jim and Bill ran
past a hill.

Can Bill pass Jim?

Bill and Jim pass
a man and his pet,
Biff.

Will Jim let Bill
pass him?

The cliff!
The cliff!

Yip!
Yip!

"The cliff! The cliff!"
The man did yell.

Bill fell. It was a bad spill.

Bill hit his hip and bit his lip.
Bill is in a big mess.

44

The man and Biff yell "help."

Help!
Help!

Yip!
Yip!

Will Jim help Bill?
Yes, Jim will.

Jim ran fast.

The man ran fast. Bill is a mess.
The man and Jim will help fix Bill.

The man can help
Jim lift Bill.

Jim and the man did help Bill.
It is not bad. Bill wins!
Jim Wins! The man wins!

MILEPOST 10 ĭ INITIAL DATE

ten nis   pic nic
tennis   picnic

Kim's Big Win

Kim will miss it!

Ben will hit it to Kim. Kim will get it back to Ben. Bam! It went fast. Ben did help Kim.

Ben hit it back. Kim ran fast. Kim hit it! Bam! It hit the net! Kim is sad.

Kim is in the tennis camp. It is the big tennis test.

Kim has a grip. Kim hit it fast. Bam! It went. Kim has a big win!

It is a big blast. Kim is glad.

Ben is Kim's fan. Ben did help Kim! Ben did a quick jig. Kick! Kick!

Kim will rest. Ben will fix the mix. Ben has a big pan. Ben has ten eggs, ham, and milk in the pan. Ben will mix it and mix it.

Ben will tip the can. It is in.

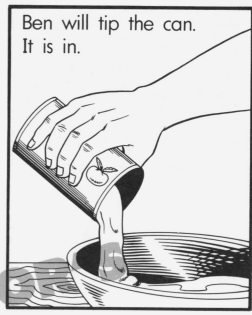

Ben can fix it.

Ben will fill the tin pan. It is in. Ben has a sip. M-m-m-m.

M-m-m-m.

Ben and Kim have a picnic. Yip, yip went Ripp.

Yip
Yip

Kim will give Ben a kiss! Ben is glad Sis had a win!

1 (if) in sip	**2** yip sit (miss)	**3** (it) Biff lip	**4** six fill (Sis)
5 pig (Jim) did	**6** pin (is) big	**7** (milk) bib hill	**8** kick (hit) jig
9 (Ripp) his lid	**10** him fit (give)	**11** dig his (did)	**12** (will) bit quick
13 mitt digs (tin)	**14** Jill (Jim) will	**15** (Biff) miss kiss	**16** (pig) him big
17 will milk (fit)	**18** whiz (tip) lift	**19** gift (spill) kiss	**20** it (is) in

Tell the student to circle the word you call in each box. Have him underline the word referred to in the comprehension question. See manual.

Mastery Score

Word Recognition

Number Correct _____ x 5 = [___] %

Mastery Score

Word Comprehension

Number Correct _____ x 5 = [___] %

1. Bill fell. It was a bad spill.

A ○ B ● C ○ D ○ E ○

A

2. The man and Biff yell for help.

A ○ B ○ C ● D ○ E ○

3. Bill and Jim pass a man and his pet, Biff.

A ○ B ○ C ○ D ● E ○

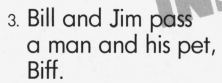

B

4. Bill is a mess. The man will help fix Bill.

A ● B ○ C ○ D ○ E ○

C

D

5. Bill wins! Jim wins! The man wins!

A ○ B ○ C ○ D ○ E ●

E

6. Kim is in the tennis camp. It is the big tennis test.

A ○　B ○　C ●　D ○　E ○

A

7. Ben is Kim's fan. Ben is in the stands. Ben did a quick jig.

A ●　B ○　C ○　D ○　E ○

B

8. Kim will give Ben a kiss! Ben is glad Sis had a win!

A ○　B ○　C ○　D ○　E ●

C

9. Kim will rest. Ben will fix the mix.

A ○　B ○　C ○　D ●　E ○

10. Ben and Kim have a picnic. Yip, yip, went Ripp.

A ○　B ●　C ○　D ○　E ○

D

E

Mastery Score

Story Comprehension

Total Correct _____ x 10 = [%   ]

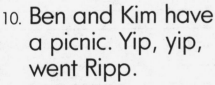

1 top   *top*

2 hog

3 Tom

4 got

5 cob

6 Don

7 rob

8 ox

9 lot

10 Bob

11 dot

12 hop

13 fox

14 God

15 tot

16 fog

17 box

18 not

19 nod

20 sob

21 mop

22 on

23 cot

24 job

25 pot

26 rod

27 hot

28 dog

29 rot

30 jog

CAN READ	CAN WRITE	CAN SPELL
INITIAL DATE	INITIAL DATE	INITIAL DATE

31 pop

32 mom

33 log

34 tom-tom

35 doll

36 odd

37 Todd

38 boss

39 Oz

40 pod

41 sock

42 clock

43 lock

44 block

45 blocks

46 rock

47 spot

48 stop

49 from

50 off

51 toss

52 lost

53 dock

54 soft

55 floss

56 Doc

57 gone

58 said (sĕd).

59 to

60 of (ov)

CAN READ

INITIAL   DATE

CAN WRITE

INITIAL   DATE

CAN SPELL

INITIAL   DATE

Jock and Jill

Jock got Jill a big rock. It is in a red box. It has a pink ribbon on it.

Jock met Jill on the dock.

Jill got a kiss. Jill got the box. Jill got the big rock.

Jill and Jock lock hands. Jock got a big kiss. . .

. .and fell off the dock.

Jill bent and held his hand. Jill will give his neck a kiss. Jock is still the best.

Lost!

Dot digs in the bag, but it is not in Dot's bag.

It is not on Dot's bed. "It is odd," said Dot. "Not in the bag and not on the bed."

Dot bent to dig in the desk. "It is not in the desk. It is gone," said Dot.

Todd will help Dot. It had been in Dot's bag. The bag had been on the bed. It is not in the bag. It is not on the bed. It is lost.

Todd got the big box. "It is not in the box," said Todd.

Todd went to his cab. "It is not in the cab," said Todd.

Todd went to Dot's hot rod. It is not in the hot rod.

Is it at Dot's job? Todd will jog to Dot's job. It is ten blocks. Todd's dog will jog.

Dot's boss is at the job. Todd will ask Dot's boss. Dot's boss did not nod yes. It is not at Dot's job! "Dot will sob," said Todd.

Todd got hot. It is a hot jog. It is ten blocks. Todd did not stop. Todd will jog back to tell Dot. Todd's dog can jog fast!

Dot is hot. Dot is sad. Todd tells Dot it is not at Dot's job. Dot yells, "It is still lost!" Todd tells Dot not to sob. Todd gives a peck on the lips and a pat on the back.

But Dot is still mad and sad!

Jan ran to Dot. Jan will give Dot a kiss. Jan will give Dot a gift.

Jan's gift is a fan. Jan will hand it to Dot. It can fan Dot.

Tax Bill

Dot held Jan's fan. Dot can yell and sob. "It is not lost! It is not lost!" Jan's fan is Dot's lost tax bill! The tax bill is not lost!

The tax bill! It is not lost!

Jan did help Dot. Dot did a jig. Todd will kiss Jan. Jan did help Todd and Dot.

ŏ

1 (fox) top spot	2 rob (box) hog	3 (God) hop dot	4 hot got (log)
5 doll (dog) jog	6 Mom stop (hot)	7 not (pot) cot	8 (hop) stop log
9 rob hog (from)	10 ox (lot) Oz	11 (Todd) cot tom-tom	12 (on) lot top
13 log (sock) dog	14 not pop (odd)	15 lock clock (rock)	16 odd on (doll)
17 pop (spot) stop	18 rock (not) lock	19 fox (top) box	20 sock (blocks) pot

Tell the student to circle the word you call in each box. Have him underline the word referred to in the comprehension question. See manual.

Mastery Score

Word Recognition

Number Correct _____ x 5 = [%]

Mastery Score

Word Comprehension

Number Correct _____ x 5 = [%]

1. Jock got Jill a big rock. It is in a red box.

   A ○   B ○   C ○   D ●   E ○

2. Jill bent and held his hand. Jock is still the best.

   A ○   B ○   C ○   D ○   E ●

3. Jock fell off the dock.

   A ○   B ●   C ○   D ○   E ○

4. Jock met Jill on the dock.

   A ●   B ○   C ○   D ○   E ○

5. Dot digs in the bag, but it is not in Dot's bag.

   A ○   B ○   C ●   D ○   E ○

A

B

C

D

E

6. Dot's boss is at the job. Todd will ask Dot's boss.

A ○ B ○ C ○ D ● E ○

A Tax Bill

7. Jan's gift is a fan. Jan will hand it to Dot.

A ● B ○ C ○ D ○ E ○

B

C

8. Todd went to Dot's hot rod. It is not in the hot rod.

A ○ B ○ C ● D ○ E ○

D

9. Jan did help Dot. Dot did a quick jig. Todd will kiss Jan.

A ○ B ○ C ○ D ○ E ●

E

10. Dot held Jan's fan. It is not lost! Jan's fan is Dot's lost tax bill!

A ○ B ● C ○ D ○ E ○

Story Comprehension

Total Correct _____ x 10 =

Mastery Score

_____ %

1 gum *gum*

2 rug

3 us

4 Gus

5 bug

6 fun

7 mug

8 up

9 nut

10 bun

11 cup

12 cups

13 bus

14 hug

15 dug

16 hum

17 plum

18 rut

19 run

20 bud

21 sun

22 mud

23 hut

24 tub

25 but

26 tug

27 gun

28 pup

29 cut

30 buzz

CAN READ	CAN WRITE	CAN SPELL
INITIAL DATE	INITIAL DATE	INITIAL DATE

MILEPOST 13

ŭ

31 mutt

32 fuzz

33 puff

34 dull

35 fuss

36 dump

37 lump

38 jump

39 bump

40 drum

41 duck

42 stuck

43 truck

44 luck

45 putt

46 must

47 dust

48 snug

49 gulp

50 jug

51 rust

52 stuff

53 cuff

54 huff

55 gull

56 hull

57 Russ

58 gust

69 sub

60 pump

CAN READ	CAN WRITE	CAN SPELL
INITIAL DATE	INITIAL DATE	INITIAL DATE

Bud's Dump Truck

Bud has a dump truck. It is red, and it is not big.

"The dump truck has a lot of mud on it," said Bud. The truck is dull. It has dust on it. Gum is stuck on it. Bud must get it off his dump truck.

Bud's kid is Max. Max will help Bud. Max will dust in the cab of the truck. Max will get the dust off the fuzz of the truck rug.

Bud got Max a glass of pop. Max must not gulp it. Bud got Max a hot dog. Bud got Max a cup of nuts. Max is glad. Bud is his dad and his pal.

Tubbs is Bud's dog. Tubbs is a mutt. Tubbs ran to get a duck. But the duck ran to the pond. Off it went to swim.

Tubbs cannot get the duck. Tubbs is mad. Tubbs dug in the mud. Yuck! Lots of mud.

Tubbs is in the hot sun. Tubbs snaps at a big bug. The big bug said, "Buzz," and went up fast. Tubbs got snug on the rug of the truck.

Tubbs has a nap in the sun. Tum, tum, tum! Max can drum. Max said, "Tubbs can buff the truck and drum and nap!" Bud said, "Yes, Tubbs is the best of pals."

65

Word Recognition & Comprehension

1	2	3	4
<u>sun</u> (rub) mud	(bug) nut tub	<u>bus</u> Gus (cup)	<u>hum</u> (mug) but

5	6	7	8
(fun) dug <u>cut</u>	<u>up</u> (us) but	duck <u>bun</u> (fuss)	cup <u>dump</u> (tug)

9	10	11	12
rug <u>buzz</u> (pup)	(run) bud <u>gulp</u>	fuzz (drum) <u>snug</u>	(dug) bug bun

13	14	15	16
(hut) <u>stuck</u> gum	fun <u>mud</u> (nut)	<u>cups</u> dust (us)	(truck) <u>umbrella</u> jump

17	18	19	20
dull <u>tub</u> (cut)	(hum) <u>jump</u> snug	<u>must</u> puff (duck)	(puff) <u>fuss</u> fuzz

Tell the student to circle the word you call in each box. Have him underline the word referred to in the comprehension question. See manual.

Mastery Score

Word Recognition

Number Correct _____ x 5 = [%   ]

Mastery Score

Word Comprehension

Number Correct _____ x 5 = [%   ]

66

Story Comprehension

1. Bud has a dump truck.
   It is red.

   A ○ B ○ C ○ D ○ E ●

2. Bud's kid is Max.
   Max will help Bud.

   A ○ B ○ C ● D ○ E ○

3. Tum, Tum, Tum!
   Max can drum.

   A ○ B ● C ○ D ○ E ○

INSTRUCTOR'S COPY

4. Tubbs is Bud's dog.
   Tubbs is a mutt.

   A ● B ○ C ○ D ○ E ○

5. Tubbs snaps at a big
   bug. The big bug
   said, "Buzz," and went
   up fast.

   A ○ B ○ C ○ D ● E ○

6. Tubbs is mad.
   Tubbs dug in the mud.

   A   B   C   D   E
   ○   ○   ○   ●   ○

7. Bud got Max a glass
   of pop. Max must
   not gulp it.

   A   B   C   D   E
   ●   ○   ○   ○   ○

A

8. "Tubbs can buff the
   truck and drum and
   nap!" Bud said.

   A   B   C   D   E
   ○   ●   ○   ○   ○

B

9. Tubbs ran to get a
   duck. But the duck ran
   to the pond.

   A   B   C   D   E
   ○   ○   ●   ○   ○

C

10. Max will get the dust
    off the fuzz of the
    truck rug.

    A   B   C   D   E
    ○   ○   ○   ○   ●

D

E

Story Comprehension

Total Correct _____ x 10 = [   ] %

Mastery Score

1 hand hand
2 vest
3 stick
4 clock
5 truck
6 lamp
7 nest
8 sick
9 dots
10 duck
11 tack
12 tent
13 hill
14 frog
15 pump

16 rest
17 snack
18 Dick
19 must
20 damp
21 bent
22 sift
23 fond
24 rust
25 land
26 test
27 mend
28 hunt
29 hump
30 fact

CAN READ

INITIAL   DATE

CAN WRITE

INITIAL   DATE

CAN SPELL

INITIAL   DATE

1 fast _fast_

2 send

3 Jack

4 kept

5 just

6 pill

7 wept

8 mask

9 belt

10 milk

11 spot

12 bulb

13 sand

14 elf

15 fist

16 block

17 jump

18 camp

19 desk

20 gift

21 pond

22 dust

23 band

24 from

25 melt

26 ask

27 grand

28 gulp

29 lump

30 went

CAN READ	CAN WRITE	CAN SPELL
INITIAL DATE	INITIAL DATE	INITIAL DATE

1 list   list
2 swam
3 silk
4 sock
5 best
6 dump
7 back
8 limp
9 spend
10 sulk
11 bend
12 lift
13 bump
14 pick
15 drip

16 glass
17 twist
18 hunk
19 junk
20 plug
21 blast
22 brass
23 pic nic
   picnic
24 can not
   cannot
25 hot dog
26 hot rod
27 ten nis
   tennis

CAN READ	CAN WRITE	CAN SPELL
INITIAL DATE	INITIAL DATE	INITIAL DATE

Hot Rod Fix-it Pit Stop

Doc is the boss of the Hot Rod Pit Stop. Dick and Fran help Doc fix hot rods.

Bob has a hot rod. The stick is off. The back tag is off. It has to have gas. Can Doc fix it? Yes Doc can.

It is a hunk of junk.

Dick will fill the tank.

Bob's gas tank is bad. Doc must fix it. Drip! Drip! Drip!

Fran will jack it up. Up and up went Bob's hot rod.

Dick has a rag and Dick will mop up the gas. Doc will fix the gas tank.

Dick has a sack. The sack has rags in it. Dick hands Doc a rag. Doc will rub his hands on it.

The trunk lid is up. It will not lock. Doc can fix it. Doc will fix the lid and the lock.

Doc will fix the dent.

Fran will fix the back tag.

The ragtop has a rip. Doc will mend it.

It will not gap and let the wind in.

"Jack it up, Dick!" Dick will fix the flat. It had a tack in it. Dick can mend the flat. It will get a plug. "Let's pump it up."

Next, Dick must wax and buff it. The wax will get the spots off. Dab and rub. Rub and scrub. Dick will wax it.

"Twist the button, Fran! The flip flops must stop."

The glass has a spot. Dick will get the spot off the glass. The glass is not bad. The black spot is off.

Bob can get his hot rod.

Did Doc fix the plugs?

Yes, and the bill is not bad.

Bob pats Doc on the back.

Off went Bob in his hot rod.

It is not a hunk of junk.

It is just grand!

The Junk Stop

The Best For Less

1021

Lil said, "The Junk Stop is the best!" Lil and Matt went in. Matt will get a desk. Lil has a list.

The Junk Stop has a lot on Lil's list: silk socks, a vest, a clock, and a big lamp. Lil is glad.

Matt went to get a desk. A tan desk had a red tag on it. "It will not cost a lot," Matt tells Lil.

Matt said, "The tan desk is just grand." Matt tells Lil to rub a hand on it...not a spot of rust, and not a bump! Matt and Lil will get it.

A man must help Matt pick it up.

It will fit in Matt's van.

Matt did not have to spend a lot. Matt will give six big bills to the man. The man will help Matt lift the desk in the van, and Matt will give him a tip.

The clock and Lil's bag went in the van. The men lift the desk up and in. Lil will get the lamp in.

Off went Lil and Matt in the van. Lil said, "Let's stop and get hot dogs." "Yes," said Matt. Matt went to the Snack Hut and got hot dogs. Off Matt and Lil went, but not fast. The desk and lamp must not tip.

Lil will help Matt lift up the desk. In it went. Lil will not drop it. Lil is big and Lil can lift it.

Matt will lift the desk and fix the rug. Matt will tack the rug. Tap, tap, tap!

Lil will fix the lamp and dust the desk.

It is the best desk.

Matt and Lil must rest. Matt and Lil had fun at The Junk Stop!

The Jazz Band

Les has a jazz band.
Les can pick and strum.
His hand is fast. Les
is the boss of the band.

Rat, tat, tat. It is Mack. Mack has a drum and sticks. "Hit it, Mack!" said Les. Mack and Les can drum and strum.

Hit it, Mack!

The band has lots of brass. Bev has a trumpet. It is brass. Bev can help Les and Mack have a jazz hit.

Bev will yell to Les, "Not soft, Les! Hit it!" Les will hit it.

Not soft, Les! Hit it!

Les and Mack have a blast.

Les said, "The band is grand. It is a jazz hit."

The band is grand. It is a jazz hit.

Bev said, "Not bad! It is the best hit yet."

Not bad! It is the best hit yet!

Les said, "Give the band a hand!"

Give the trumpet a hand!

Give the drum a hand!

The fans clap and clap. It is a fact. The jazz band is the best.

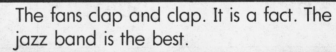

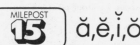

1 lump _lamp_ (land)	2 (stick) _snack_ spend	3 _sand_ send (sock)	4 lift (list) _limp_
5 dust (dump) _dots_	6 just _jump_ (Jack)	7 (melt) mend _milk_	8 test (tack) _tent_
9 _Dick_ duck desk	10 hunt hump _hand_	11 grand (gulp) _gift_	12 best (bend) _band_
13 (truck) _clock_ stick	14 _belt_ (block) bulb	15 _fact_ fast (fist)	16 _sock_ sick (sift)
17 (must) mask _mend_	18 pill (pick) _pond_	19 (damp) dump _duck_	20 from _frog_ (fond)

Tell the student to circle the word you call in each box. Have him underline the word referred to in the comprehension question. See manual.

Mastery Score

Word Recognition

Number Correct _____ x 5 = [___ %]

Mastery Score

Word Comprehension

Number Correct _____ x 5 = [___ %]

1. Bob's gas tank is bad.
Doc must fix it.
Drip! Drip! Drip!

A ○ B ○ C ● D ○ E ○

A

2. The ragtop has a rip.
Doc will mend it.
"It will not gap and
let the wind in."

A ○ B ○ C ○ D ○ E ●

B

3. Dick must wax and
buff it. The wax will
get the spots off.

A ○ B ○ C ○ D ● E ○

C

D

4. Off went Bob in
his hot rod. "It is
not a hunk of junk."
"It is just grand!"

A ● B ○ C ○ D ○ E ○

It will not gap and
let the wind in.
E

5. Matt went to get a
desk. A tan desk had
a red tag on it.

A ○ B ● C ○ D ○ E ○

6. Off went Lil and Matt in the van. Lil said, "Let's stop and get hotdogs." "Yes," said Matt.

A ○ B ○ C ● D ○ E ○

A

7. Matt will lift the desk and fix the rug. Matt will tack the rug.

A ○ B ○ C ○ D ○ E ●

B

8. Bev has a trumpet. It is brass. Bev can help Les and Mack have a jazz hit.

A ○ B ○ C ○ D ● E ○

C

9. "Hit it Mack," said Les. Mack and Les can drum and strum.

A ○ B ● C ○ D ○ E ○

D

E

10. The fans clap and clap. It is a fact. The jazz band is the best.

A ● B ○ C ○ D ○ E ○

Mastery Score

Story Comprehension

Total Correct _____ x 10 = _____ %